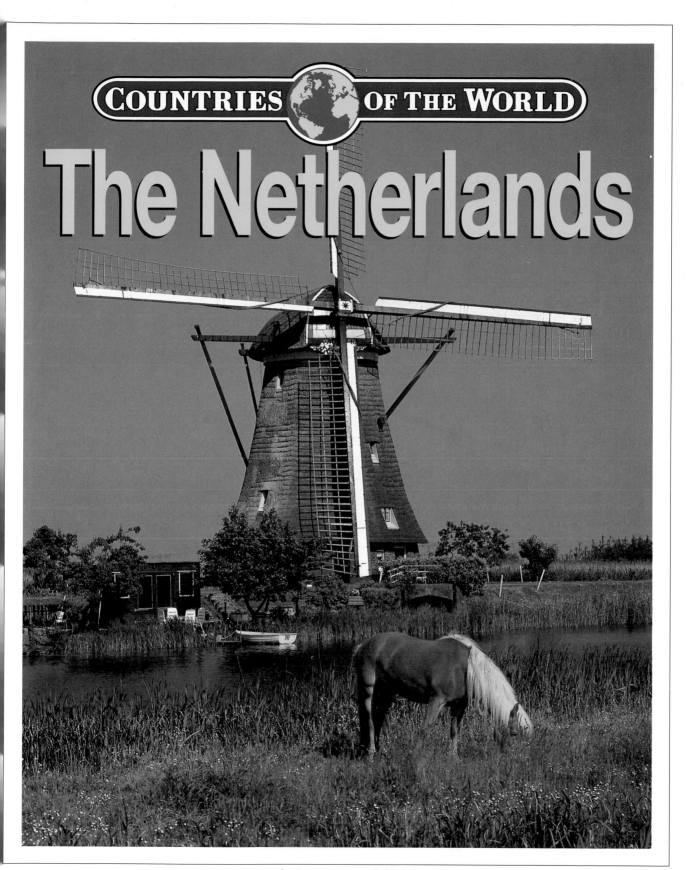

COUNTRIES OF THE WORLD

The Netherlands

Gareth Stevens Publishing
A WORLD ALMANAC EDUCATION GROUP COMPANY

About the Author: Born in Mauritius, Roseline NgCheong-Lum has lived in Europe, North America, and Southeast Asia. She has traveled extensively in Europe and has a deep interest in various European cultures. She is the author of several books for children.

Written by
ROSELINE NGCHEONG-LUM

Edited by
SELINA KUO

Edited in the U.S. by
PATRICIA LANTIER
MONICA RAUSCH

Designed by
GEOSLYN LIM

Picture research by
SUSAN JANE MANUEL

First published in North America in 2001 by
Gareth Stevens Publishing
A World Almanac Education Group Company
330 West Olive Street, Suite 100
Milwaukee, Wisconsin 53212

Please visit our web site at:
www.garethstevens.com
For a free color catalog describing
Gareth Stevens' list of high-quality books
and multimedia programs, call
1-800-542-2595 (USA) or
1-800-461-9120 (CANADA).
Gareth Stevens Publishing's
Fax: (414) 332-3567.

© **TIMES MEDIA PRIVATE LIMITED 2001**
Originated and designed by
Times Editions
An imprint of Times Media Private Limited
A member of the Times Publishing Group
Times Centre, 1 New Industrial Road
Singapore 536196
http://www.timesone.com.sg/te

Library of Congress Cataloging-in-Publication Data
NgCheong-Lum, Roseline, 1962-
The Netherlands / by Roseline NgCheong-Lum.
p. cm. — (Countries of the world)
Includes bibliographical references and index.
ISBN 0-8368-2336-2 (lib. bdg.)
1. Netherlands — Juvenile literature. [1. Netherlands] I. Countries of the world (Milwaukee, Wis.)
DJ18.N47   2001
949.2—dc21   2001020535

Printed in Malaysia

1 2 3 4 5 6 7 8 9 05 04 03 02 01

PICTURE CREDITS
Agence de Presse ANA: 34
Archive Photos: 72 (bottom), 81
Benelux Press: 66, 67, 68, 69
Canadian Press: 65, 78, 84, 85 (bottom)
Victor Englebert: 29
Focus Team — Italy: 4, 41, 42, 44, 48, 49
Fraser Photos: 79, 85 (top)
Robert Fried: 5, 23, 72 (top)
Hulton Getty: 10, 11, 12, 15 (top and center), 53 (both), 76 (both), 77, 80, 83
Globe Press: 13, 17
Dave G. Houser: 20 (both), 31, 33 (bottom), 55
The Hutchinson Library: 9
Keith Mundy: 57, 58
Dave Simson: 24, 28, 36, 39, 47, 74
Topham Picturepoint: cover, 2, 3 (bottom), 14, 15 (bottom), 16, 19, 21, 25, 27, 30, 32, 45, 51, 52, 56, 59, 63, 64, 73, 82, 87
Travel Ink Photo and Feature Library: 33 (top), 70
Trip Photo Library: 1, 3 (top and center), 6, 7, 8, 18, 22, 26, 35, 37, 38, 40, 43, 46, 50, 54, 60, 61, 62, 71, 75, 89, 91

Digital Scanning by Superskill Graphics Pte Ltd

Contents

AN OVERVIEW OF THE NETHERLANDS

The Netherlands is defined by water. The North Sea borders the country on two sides, and a large part of the land is below sea level. Land reclamation has always been important in Dutch life and history. To make more of the country inhabitable, the Dutch constantly reclaim submerged land. They have been draining marshes and lakes, adding more earth, and building dams since medieval times. The ceaseless fight against encroaching waters has hardened the Dutch character and encouraged great inventiveness. Throughout history, the Netherlands has produced outstanding artists, philosophers, scientists, and scholars. Many modern Dutch engineering projects are technical triumphs, and the Dutch economy is one of the most advanced in the world.

Opposite: **The canals that flow through and around Amsterdam add character and flavor to the city.**

Below: **Located in Noord-Holland, the Central Railway Station in Amsterdam is a major landmark.**

THE FLAG OF THE NETHERLANDS

The Dutch flag, or tricolor, was first raised in the second half of the sixteenth century during the country's long fight for independence from Spain. At that time, the Dutch were led by Prince William I of Orange, and the tricolor consisted of three horizontal bands of orange, white, and blue. The red, white, and blue version that represents the country today emerged in the early seventeenth century. By 1660, flags bearing the orange band had become very rare. Queen Wilhelmina made the red-white-blue tricolor the official flag of the Netherlands in 1937.

Geography

Bordered by the North Sea to the north and west, Germany to the east and southeast, and Belgium to the south, the Netherlands is a flat country with few hills and no mountains. The Netherlands occupies an area of 16,031 square miles (41,532 square kilometers), but the country's land area frequently increases through land reclamation.

The Provinces

The Netherlands has twelve provinces. The most well-known among them are Noord-Holland, Zuid-Holland, and Utrecht, all of which lie in the western, most urbanized part of the country. The landscape in this area consists of flat, agricultural regions cut by trenches and canals. The area also contains the Randstad, a densely populated region that includes The Hague, Rotterdam, Utrecht, and other urban centers.

The southern provinces are Zeeland, Noord-Brabant, and Limburg. Zeeland sits at the delta of three great rivers — the Rhine, the Schelde, and the Maas. The country's largest province,

THE DELTA PROJECT

Prone to frequent flooding, the low-lying areas of Zeeland were secured in 1986 with the Delta Project, a large-scale land reclamation project. *(A Closer Look, page 50)*

RIVERS, LAKES, AND CANALS

Water is a regular feature of the Netherlands; approximately one-fourth of the country's land lies below sea level. Three major European rivers flow into the Netherlands — the Rhine, Maas, and Schelde rivers. The largest lake in the country is the IJsselmeer, a freshwater lake that formed when a dam was erected to close off the southern part of what used to be Zuiderzee, an inlet of the North Sea.

Left: Although one of the most urbanized parts of the country, Zuid-Holland has not lost its rustic appeal.

Above: **The sheep on this farm in Utrecht graze on a lot less land than those sheep raised in the northern Netherlands.**

Noord-Brabant, has a landscape different from the rest of the country, with alternating plots of woodland and open fields. Limburg, the southernmost province, extends into Belgium. The country's highest point, Vaalserberg, stands at 1,053 feet (321 meters). It is located in southern Limburg.

The eastern provinces are Gelderland, Flevoland, and Overijssel. The Dutch refer to Gelderland as the "bad land" because the area is not very fertile and remained deserted for many years. Today, Gelderland is a popular holiday camping destination. Established in 1986, Flevoland, the newest Dutch province, consists entirely of reclaimed land. Overijssel is an industrial and agricultural region sectioned by lakes and canals.

The provinces of Drenthe, Groningen, and Friesland form the northern part of the country. Drenthe, an agricultural area, is the most sparsely populated of the Dutch provinces. The key feature of Groningen is the famous university town, also called Groningen. Friesland originally belonged to an ancient kingdom, Frisia, and, until the sixteenth century, was not a part of the Netherlands.

NETHERLANDS ANTILLES

The Netherlands Antilles consists of four islands in the Caribbean Sea — Bonaire, Curaçao, Sint Eustatius, and Saba — as well as the southern part of the island of Sint Maarten. Part of the Netherlands since 1954, the islands' main industry is tourism.

Mild Summers and Chilly Winters

Located close to the North Sea, the Netherlands has a cool, maritime climate moderated by ocean currents and offshore winds. In winter, the average temperature hovers at 35° Fahrenheit (2° Celsius). Temperatures rarely reach freezing point, but a stiff inland wind often blows over low-lying areas, making the climate seem much colder. The country receives an average of twenty-eight days of snow every year. Ponds and canals are also known to freeze about once every three or four years, when winter is particularly severe.

In summer, the average temperature is 63° F (17° C). The Netherlands generally receives little sunshine. Skies are usually cloudy, and the average amount of rainfall is 31 inches (79 centimeters) a year. The driest season is spring, when flowers bloom and tourists flock to the country.

Left: **These children in Amsterdam are doing their best to have fun during a particularly icy winter.**

Plants and Animals

The Netherlands is best known for its flowers. In addition to the tulip, which is the national flower, hyacinths, gladioli, and narcissi grow in abundance and are exported to countries all over the world. In spring, flowers adorn windowsills and gardens throughout the Netherlands. Fruit trees, particularly those bearing apples and pears, and garden vegetables, such as tomatoes and peas, also grow well in Dutch soil. Forests occupy approximately 8 percent of Dutch territories and include beech, oak, pine, and birch trees.

The small amount of forest in the Netherlands has led to limited wildlife. Most of the country's animals are small mammals common to the rest of Europe. Squirrels, foxes, wild boar, badgers, and deer roam the woodlands and nature reserves. The Netherlands is also home to hawks, swans, ducks, geese, and cormorants, or diving birds with long necks and throat pouches.

Cattle are raised on farms throughout the Netherlands. About one-third of the country's lush, green polders, or areas of reclaimed land protected by dikes, support dairy cows, especially the famous black-and-white Holstein and the Frisian varieties.

Above: **Raised for their wool and meat, domesticated sheep graze on farmland throughout the Netherlands.**

ENDANGERED

Several species of fish, reptiles, and amphibians in the Netherlands face extinction because of water pollution. The Dutch government and private organizations have created nature reserves to protect these and other animal species. Well-known reserves include the Naardermeer in Amsterdam, the Hoge Veluwe National Park in Arnhem, and the Ostvaardersplassen in southern Flevoland.

9

History

Evidence of human settlement in the Netherlands dates back about 250,000 years. Not much, however, is known about the early peoples of the region. Around 4600 B.C., tribes began to develop agricultural settlements in the region of present-day Limburg. By the first century B.C., various Germanic and Celtic groups were living in the Netherlands.

The Roman and Frankish Empires

When the Romans arrived in the region in the mid-first century B.C., they conquered the territories south of the Rhine with ease. North of the river, however, the Germanic Frisians resisted Roman conquest. Roman power began to decline in the mid-third century A.D., and, by 407, Germanic tribes had defeated the Romans in the Netherlands. A Germanic tribe called the Franks soon took control of the Netherlands, introducing the Christian religion. The Frisians in the north remained independent until 734, when they were defeated by the Franks.

Charlemagne and the Holy Roman Empire

In 800, Frankish king Charlemagne became the Holy Roman emperor, the ruler of an empire that stretched from southern Italy to Denmark and included the Netherlands. After Charlemagne's death in 814, Frankish power began to weaken. The death of Charlemagne's son Louis the Pious in 840 sparked years of infighting among Louis' three sons, and Frankish rule eventually came to an end. From the 900s to the mid-1300s, most of the modern Netherlands came under the rule of the king of Germany, who was also the Holy Roman emperor. The German government, however, had many internal problems, and the real power rested with the bishops and noblemen who each controlled smaller territories called counties. In the fifteenth century, the county of Holland fell to the dukes of Burgundy, a French royal house. In 1473, Burgundian duke Charles the Bold sought to control the rest of the Netherlands but was unsuccessful. When he died in 1477, his daughter Mary took over. She married Maximilian of Austria, the son and heir to the Holy Roman emperor at that time. In 1504, the Netherlands rejoined the Holy Roman Empire.

Opposite: **An artist's impression of one of several Frankish wars in the 300s that led to the ultimate conquest of the Netherlands.**

HOLLAND OR THE NETHERLANDS?

Holland was the dominant province of the Netherlands between the twelfth and nineteenth centuries. A military, cultural, administrative, and economic center, Holland came to stand for the entire country. The historic province of Holland was divided into Noord-Holland and Zuid-Holland in 1840.

Below: **Frankish king Charlemagne was a powerful ruler. None of his successors, however, could hold his great kingdom together.**

Left: This illustration is an artist's impression of one of the many victorious battles fought by William I of Orange. Although William I, Count of Nassau, was assassinated in 1584, the resistance against Spanish rule continued under his son Maurice of Nassau. After Maurice's death in 1625, his half-brother Frederick Henry led the Dutch. Finally, in 1648, the Spanish officially recognized the independence of the Netherlands.

The United Provinces

By the early 1500s, many European scholars had begun to question the power that the Roman Catholic Church had in influencing politics and daily life. Reformation, a Protestant movement against the Roman Catholic Church, started in 1517 and, over time, drew many Dutch supporters. King Philip II of Spain, a Catholic, decreed that all Protestant uprisings must be suppressed, but Prince William I of Orange led the Dutch resistance against the Spanish forces. In 1579, the provinces of Friesland, Holland, Gelderland, Groningen, Overijssel, Utrecht, and Zeeland united under a treaty that voiced a desire to break away from Spanish rule. The provinces came to be known as the United Provinces of the Netherlands and were the earliest form of a Dutch nation. Today, 1579 is regarded as the country's date of independence.

The Golden Age

The seventeenth century was the Golden Age of the Netherlands. Because of its strategic location, Amsterdam became a center for trade in Europe. The economy boomed, and the newly formed Dutch East India and Dutch West India companies secured profitable trade routes throughout Europe and East Asia. The Netherlands also set up colonies in Sri Lanka, South Africa, Indonesia, Brazil, and the West Indies, where valuable goods, such as spices and gold, were produced and mined.

THE MONARCHY

The Dutch monarchy today is a legacy of the House of Orange. Although the House of Orange has a history that dates back to the Middle Ages, it was only after playing an important role in securing the country's independence that the family became royalty.

(A Closer Look, page 58)

The country's liberal attitude toward trade and religion attracted a surge of Protestant and Jewish immigrants from all over Europe, many of whom were already world-class merchants or industrialists. Dutch culture and art also flourished in this era, and the country produced great scientists, painters, and philosophers.

Slow Decline

Toward the end of the eighteenth century, the Netherlands was increasingly burdened by disputes with the English and the French. The fourth Anglo-Dutch War (1780–1784) greatly weakened the Netherlands, giving French troops the opportunity to invade in 1795. The Republic of the United Provinces hence became part of the French-controlled Batavian Republic for the next eleven years. To prevent French control of Dutch colonies, the Netherlands allowed Britain to occupy many of them. Although the Netherlands regained control of some of its colonies after the Napoleonic wars, Dutch trade declined greatly.

In 1813, the Dutch rebelled against French rule, and in 1815, Prince William VI was made the first king of the United Kingdom of the Netherlands, which included present-day Belgium and Luxembourg. Belgium eventually gained independence in 1830 and Luxembourg in 1839. In the second half of the nineteenth century, the Dutch monarchy's power was greatly reduced, and the Dutch people gained a greater say in government.

THE KINGDOM OF HOLLAND (1806–1810)

The French invasion of the Netherlands in 1795 was led by French emperor Napoleon Bonaparte. In 1806, the Batavian Republic was renamed the Kingdom of Holland, with Napoleon's younger brother Louis Bonaparte as king. Louis, however, sided with the Dutch and frequently ignored his brother's commands. In 1810, Napoleon dethroned him and reabsorbed the Netherlands into the French empire.

Left: Built during the peak of Dutch trade and civilization in the 1600s, the Dutch East India House in Amsterdam is a magnificent building.

From the World Wars to the Present

Queen Wilhelmina ruled the Netherlands from 1890 to 1948. She declared the country's neutrality in World War I (1914–1918). When World War II broke out in 1939, the Netherlands again declared its neutrality, but this move did not stop the Germans from invading the country in 1940. Rotterdam was bombed to the ground, and five years of brutal occupation began. Queen Wilhelmina refused to collaborate with the German Nazis, and she escaped to London to form a government in exile there. After the Germans surrendered in 1945, Queen Wilhelmina returned from exile and established a government more strongly democratic than before. Wilhelmina was succeeded in 1948 by her daughter Juliana, who also continued to build a democratic government. Since the 1960s, the Netherlands has pursued a policy of economic development through investment in technology. The elected governments have been a coalition of various political parties, and the current ruler is Queen Beatrix, who came to power in 1980.

Above: **Queen Juliana (r. 1948–1980) watches a horse show with her daughters, princesses Beatrix *(left)* and Irene *(right).* Princess Beatrix succeeded Queen Juliana in 1980.**

MATA HARI

To this day, no historian can say for sure if the notorious Mata Hari was indeed a spy in the epoch of World War I. The Dutch woman's colorful life has since been immortalized in a Hollywood film. Greta Garbo played Mata Hari.
(A Closer Look, page 56)

William I of Orange (1533–1584)

Also known as William the Silent, William I of Orange, Count of Nassau, was made *stadholder* (STAHD-hoh-der), or governor, of Holland, Zeeland, and Utrecht in 1559. William strongly opposed King Philip II's repression of Dutch Protestants, and in the 1570s, he led the provinces of the Netherlands in a revolt against the Spanish army. He was murdered by a Catholic in 1584, before independence could be won. A firm believer in individual freedom and tolerance, William remains an icon of liberty for the Dutch people today.

William I of Orange

Johan de Witt (1625–1672)

Johan de Witt was councillor pensionary (prime minister) from 1653 to 1672. He distrusted the princes of Orange and worked to keep them from power. A shrewd politician, de Witt guided the Dutch Republic through wars with England and Sweden and negotiated a triple alliance among the countries. When France attacked the Dutch Republic in 1672, however, public opinion turned in favor of the House of Orange, and the people of The Hague brutally murdered de Witt.

Johan de Witt

Johan Rudolf Thorbecke (1798–1872)

J. R. Thorbecke was one of the men appointed in 1848 by King William II to revise the constitution. He was largely responsible for the final version, which increased the power of the States-General and reduced that of the Dutch monarch. During his terms as the nation's prime minister (1849–1853, 1862–1866, and 1871–1872), he implemented the direct election of local governments and promoted free trade.

Queen Wilhelmina (1880–1962)

Queen Wilhelmina succeeded her father, William III, when she was ten years old. Many welfare policies were introduced during her reign. The Dutch remember Wilhelmina for her strong, moral leadership, especially during the two World Wars. During the Nazi occupation of the Netherlands, she encouraged her people to resist the Germans through Radio Orange broadcasts from England. The Dutch people welcomed her return in 1945.

Queen Wilhelmina

Government and the Economy

A Constitutional Monarchy

The Netherlands is a constitutional monarchy, which means that the head of state is a king or queen, but the constitution limits royal powers, and an act of parliament can easily abolish the monarchy. Although the ruler is largely a figurehead, laws cannot be passed without his or her signature. Since 1980, the ruler of the Netherlands has been Queen Beatrix Wilhelmina Armgard.

The Prime Minister and the States-General

Effective governmental power rests with the prime minister, who is appointed by the monarch. Assisted by two vice prime ministers, the prime minister heads the cabinet of ministers. Parliament, called the States-General, consists of members from all the different political parties. The First Chamber, or upper

VOTING

All Dutch citizens eighteen years of age and above may vote or run for general elections, although voting is not compulsory.

Below: The Dutch parliament building is located in The Hague. Although Amsterdam is the country's capital, the seat of government is in The Hague.

Left: **This memorial commemorates the establishment of the Limburg provincial government in Maastricht. In the Netherlands, provinces are further divided into municipalities, and municipal authorities are responsible for water supply, traffic, public schools, social services, health care, housing, recreation, sports, and culture. Each municipal authority consists of an elected council and a mayor appointed by the Dutch government.**

De Europese Raad vergaderde in het Gouvernement op 9 en 10 december 1991 Het Verdrag van Maastricht werd hier getekend op 7 februari 1992

house, has seventy-five members elected to four-year terms by the local governments of the twelve provinces. The Dutch people directly elect the 150 members of the Second Chamber, or lower house, to four-year terms.

Provincial Administration

Provincial authorities are responsible for environmental management, land planning, energy, social work, sports, and cultural affairs. Each provincial authority consists of an elected provincial council and a commissioner appointed by the monarch.

National Defense

Compulsory enlistment for military service was suspended in the Netherlands on January 1, 1997. From 1997 to 2000, the Dutch military system underwent reorganization, and national defense is now provided by a group of well-equipped military professionals. The defense forces are small in number, with less than 75,000 men and women, but these forces are well trained and utilize the latest technology. The armed forces consist of the Royal Netherlands Army, Royal Netherlands Navy, Royal Netherlands Air Force, and the Marechaussee, or military police, responsible for controlling the country's borders and guarding the royal palaces.

WELFARE SERVICES

The Netherlands provides one of the world's most generous social security programs.
(A Closer Look, page 68)

Agriculture

Although the Netherlands is fairly small, the country is the third largest exporter of agricultural produce in the world, after the United States and France. Almost half the country's land is devoted to agriculture, with dairy farming taking up about one-third of the polders. Cattle farms are found mostly in Friesland. Much of the country's dairy goods are exported as butter, cheese, or condensed milk.

Vegetables, such as tomatoes, cucumbers, and lettuce, are grown in hothouses. Most of these vegetables are exported to countries as far away as the United States. Fruit is grown in Gelderland, while rapeseed is cultivated for oil in Groningen, Friesland, and Flevoland.

Despite the nation's high output, only 4 percent of the Dutch workforce is employed in agriculture. Farms are usually small and family-run, passing from one generation to the next. Dutch farmers have plentiful yields because they use industrialized methods and heavy chemical fertilizers, which tend to pollute water sources. Members of the European Union (EU) have criticized these methods in recent years. Today, the Dutch farming sector stresses ecological responsibility.

FLOWERS OF THE NETHERLANDS

Dutch farmers produce various types of bulbs, including tulips, gladioli, hyacinths, and crocuses, in hothouses as well as in open fields. The most popular flowers, however, are roses. Most flowers are grown in hothouses in Noord-Holland, Zuid-Holland, and Zeeland.
(*A Closer Look, page 54*)

CHEESES OF THE NETHERLANDS

The Netherlands produces six main types of cheeses. The two most popular cheeses are Edam, which is covered in red wax, and Gouda, which is covered in yellow wax.
(*A Closer Look, page 46*)

Left: **This commercial hyacinth grower is harvesting the flowers by hand.**

Industry and Trade

The Netherlands is a highly industrialized country. Some of the world's largest multinational companies, such as Unilever and Philips, operate in the country. The petroleum sector, which includes industry heavyweights Royal Dutch Shell, British Petroleum (BP), Exxon, and Texaco, is especially strong. The manufacturing sector employs about 23 percent of the workforce and mainly produces metals, chemicals, textiles, and rubber. Shipbuilding is also a significant industry in the Netherlands.

The Netherlands has always been a major international trade center because of its strategic location. Trade contributes about 50 to 60 percent of the country's gross domestic product (GDP). More than one-third of all shipped goods bound for the EU passes through the country. Europoort, the port area between Rotterdam and the North Sea, can accommodate the deepest ocean-going ships, and Rotterdam handles the most tonnage in the world. The Netherlands' main trading partners are the EU countries, such as Germany, Belgium, and France, as well as the United States.

Above: **This futuristic building in Rotterdam is one of several World Trade Centers in the Netherlands.**

LEADING IMPORTS AND EXPORTS

Leading Dutch exports include machinery and transportation equipment, food, chemicals, and metals. The country imports mainly machinery and electrical equipment, chemicals, food and beverages, fuel, and manufactured goods.

People and Lifestyle

The Netherlands has a population of almost 16 million. A vast majority of the Dutch people are descendants of Germanic groups such as the Frisians, the Saxons, and the Franks. The Dutch, in general, are tall and fair-skinned, with light hair and eyes. About 9 percent of the Dutch population belong to ethnic minorities.

The most distinctive feature of the Dutch national character is tolerance of other people's differences. Since the late 1960s, the Netherlands has been receiving at least 60,000 immigrants every year. In the past, most immigrants came from former Dutch colonies such as Indonesia and Suriname. Today, however, Moroccans, Turks, and other European nationalities form the majority of immigrants.

REGIONAL COSTUMES

Although regional costumes are usually worn on Sundays or special occasions, some Dutch people wear their regional costumes on normal working days *(above)*.
(A Closer Look, page 60)

Left: In the Netherlands, most people have blond hair and blue eyes.

The Dutch Lifestyle

The Netherlands is a highly urbanized country, and most people live in towns. As much as one-third of the population resides in the Randstad. Most city dwellers live in town houses or apartment blocks. Many apartments are situated in big, old homes that have been divided into smaller units. In provincial towns, families live in houses with gardens.

The Dutch are very house-proud. Houses and apartments are filled with comfortable furniture, personal belongings, and travel souvenirs. Most Dutch households do not have curtains in their living rooms, allowing passersby a glimpse into their well-ordered homes. The Dutch also work hard to keep their gardens neat and filled with flowers.

City dwellers work a five-day week and generally reserve weekends for family activities and leisure pursuits. In rural areas, farmers rise at the crack of dawn to work in the fields. Weekly markets, where people exchange produce as well as local news, liven up village life.

Above: **The Dutch, especially those living in urban areas, like to spend some of their free time sitting at cafés, relaxing and chatting over drinks.**

Family Life

The family, whether headed by two adults or a single parent, plays an important role in Dutch culture and society. Although there are more and more single-parent families in the Netherlands today, their lifestyles do not vary much from two-parent families. Dutch families tend to be small, with two or three children, and do not usually include extended family members. Most older people live in their own homes or in retirement villages. The Dutch elderly usually see their children and grandchildren on weekends and during vacations. Some families head for a local resort, while others favor a camping trip in the woods.

Dutch families enjoy eating together. Most families have breakfast together before the children go to school and the adults to work. If the mother is a homemaker, then the children usually go home for lunch. Many fathers return home for lunch as well. When the school or work day is over, everyone heads home for dinner before spending the evening together talking about the day's events, playing board games, or watching television.

WADDEN ISLANDS

The five Wadden Islands have been popular holiday destinations among the Dutch people for years. Easily accessible, these nearby islands are perfect for short family vacations.
(A Closer Look, page 66)

Below: A newlywed couple greets friends in front of the town hall in Veere, Zeeland.

Women and Children

Dutch women are treated fairly by the law, as well as in society as a whole. Gender equality is enshrined in the constitution, and young women generally live their lives as they like. Although Dutch women are still not paid as much as men for the same work, the wage gap is narrower than in many other developed countries. Few women, however, secure top positions, either in the private or public sector, mainly because many women stop work once they have children. Many women see themselves first as mothers and homemakers, which explains why less than half of Dutch mothers work, and three-quarters of Dutch working mothers work on a part-time basis.

The Dutch dote on their children, and Dutch children are expected to be polite, obedient, and respectful. In fact, most children voluntarily help their parents with household chores. Parents generally raise their children with liberal values and do not practice favoritism. In the Netherlands, children are expected to be heard as well as seen, and children's views are taken into consideration when making family decisions.

Above: **Dutch women enjoy a wide variety of social and economic opportunities.**

Education

The Dutch educational system is one of the best in the world, and the Dutch population is highly literate. Education is compulsory and free for students between the ages of five and sixteen. Most schools and universities in the Netherlands are run by private organizations, including various churches.

Children aged four and below usually attend private, commercially operated nursery schools. Between the ages of five and twelve, they go to elementary school, where they concentrate on reading, writing, and mathematics. In the fourth year of elementary school, students are introduced to history, geography, science, and social studies.

Students have four types of secondary schools, or high schools, to choose from once they graduate from elementary school. Most students attend junior general high school, which lasts for four years and prepares students for senior vocational education. Senior general high school, on the other hand, lasts five years, and graduating students are qualified to work immediately afterward. Pre-vocational high schools offer four-year programs and provide students with a general education. The most competitive schools are those offering pre-university education. Their programs last for six years and prepare students for college.

Above: **The Dutch educational system is flexible and can be tailored to suit the needs and abilities of individual students.**

Higher Education

The Netherlands has thirteen universities in total. Of these, eight are state universities. The private institutions are the University of Amsterdam, Erasmus University in Rotterdam, the Free University in Amsterdam, the University of Nijmegen, and the University of Brabant in Tilburg.

Founded in 1575, Leiden University is the oldest university in the Netherlands. The second-oldest is the University of Groningen, which was established in 1614. The country's newest university is the Open University of the Netherlands, which was founded in 1984 and offers degrees, as well as vocational courses, by correspondence.

Apart from going to college, post-high school students have the option of attending any of the eighty-five institutions for higher professional learning, or polytechnics. Such institutions aim to equip students with a vocation or trade, as well as further their academic education in related fields.

DUTCH THINKERS

Erasmus was a distinguished scholar in both theology and philosophy. Grotius and Spinoza lived at a later time than Erasmus and were two of several great philosophers prominent during the country's Golden Age.
(*A Closer Look,* page 52)

Below: Founded in 1636, Utrecht University is the third-oldest university in the Netherlands.

Christianity

The Dutch Constitution guarantees freedom of religion for every resident of the country, and all the major faiths of the world are represented. The main religion is Christianity, divided into the Protestant and Catholic faiths. In general, most of the people living in northern Netherlands are Protestants, while most southerners belong to the Catholic Church. Within the Christian community, however, more Dutch people are Catholic than Protestant. Although its influence is in decline, religion still affects a Dutch family's choice of school, newspaper, leisure pursuits, political party, hospital, and pension plan.

Left: **Dutch Catholic churches are usually ornate, with intricate architectural details and decorations. Protestant churches, on the other hand, tend to be plain, with white walls and, occasionally, an organ. As church attendance has fallen drastically over the years, many churches have been converted to exhibition halls, concert halls, and even apartments.**

Dutch Catholics are among the most liberal in the world, supporting, for example, birth control and women priests. Such views often cause conflict between the Dutch Catholic Church and the Vatican, or the governing body of the Catholic Church. Dutch Protestants belong mainly to the Calvinist Church, which is further divided into the Reformed Church and the Orthodox Reformed Church. The former has twice as many members as the latter, and the latter is also more conservative.

Minority Faiths

Islam also has a following in the Netherlands, and Muslims make up about 3 percent of the population. They mainly are immigrants from Indonesia, Morocco, and Turkey. Hindus, Buddhists, and Jews account for about 2 percent of the population. Amsterdam was once known as the "Jerusalem of the West" because of the significant number of Jews who lived in the city. Today, about 25,000 Jews reside in Amsterdam.

WANING SUPPORT FOR ORGANIZED RELIGION

Over the past thirty years, organized religion in the Netherlands has been steadily declining. Today, nearly 40 percent of the Dutch people are unaffiliated with any religious group.

Language and Literature

Dutch is a Germanic language that is similar in many ways to German and English. The language is spoken throughout the country as well as in Flanders, a Belgian province, and in the Dutch Antilles. Dutch is also the basis for Afrikaans, the language of South Africa.

In print, the Dutch language is fairly uniform throughout the country, but spoken Dutch varies greatly from region to region. Dutch is a guttural language, and Dutch words are pronounced far back in the throat. One characteristic of the Dutch language is the repetition of vowels in a word, which indicates a longer sound.

The Netherlands also has many regional dialects, which are proudly retained by the respective inhabitants. In Friesland, the people speak Frisian, a distinct language. Frisian is more closely related to the English language than to Dutch and is taught in schools in Friesland as a second language.

DUTCH-INSPIRED ENGLISH WORDS

Many Dutch words have found their way into the English language. Words such as *smuggler*, *reef*, *keelhaul*, *waffle*, *coleslaw*, and *cookie* are all of Dutch origin.

EARLY DUTCH WRITERS

Heinrich von Veldeke, who lived in the twelfth century, is the earliest known writer to use a form of the Dutch language. His most famous works are *Eneit* and *Servatius*. Joost van den Vondel was one of the first Dutch writers to gain international fame. His masterpiece is a trilogy of tragedies, *Lucifer* (1654), *Adam in Exile* (1664), and *Noah* (1667).

Left: A woman in Limburg leisurely reads the morning paper over a cup of coffee.

Above: **The Dutch are avid readers and have maintained a literacy rate of 99 percent since 1979.**

Literature

Born in 1913, Simon Carmiggelt is one of the Netherlands' most famous and well-loved contemporary writers. Best remembered for his daily newspaper column, *Kronkel*, which means "twist," Carmiggelt wrote thousands of short, insightful, and usually humorous stories about everyday life. He died in 1987. Another important modern writer is Cees Nooteboom (1933–), who likes to explore the phenomenon of time in his work.

Women have always been prominent in Dutch literature. Archival materials suggest that the first woman writer was Hadewijch, who was published between the late twelfth and the early thirteenth centuries. In 1782, Elizabeth Wolff-Bekker and Aagje Deken produced *The History of Miss Sara Burgerhart*, a subtle character study inspired by the lives of both authors. In the same era, Isabella Agneta van Tuyll van Serooskerken, writing under the pen name of Belle van Zuylen, published *Le Noble*, a satirical novella, or short novel, criticizing the aristocracy. Twentieth-century women writers include Marga Minco, who writes war-related fiction, and Marie Stahlie, whose *Beast with Two Backs* (1994) investigates the ideas of conscience and integrity.

A YOUNG GIRL AND HER JOURNAL

Anne Frank was the daughter of a wealthy Jewish spice trader. Her life was much like that of any other girl until the Netherlands fell prey to the Nazi Occupation.
(A Closer Look, page 72)

Arts

Painting

Paintings produced during the Netherlands' Golden Age are treasured around the world. Before 1600, most art was religious in nature and commissioned by churches or private patrons. Two famous early painters were Jan van Eyck (1385–1441), who founded the Flemish school of painting, and Hieronymus Bosch (1450–1516), who specialized in fantastical religious images.

An excellent artist of the Golden Age was Frans Hals (1585–1666). Hals depicted children with great sensitivity and is especially famous for his group portraits. Two other great artists of the Golden Age are Jan Vermeer (1632–1675), who specialized in interior scenes, and Jacob van Ruisdael (1628–1682), the most inspiring of Dutch landscape artists.

Left: Jan Vermeer is known for his paintings of female figures who are often performing simple tasks. He painted this portrait of a girl wearing a turban in 1665.

Music

The Dutch people are very fond of music, and many families have at least one member who can play a musical instrument. The most famous Dutch composer is Jan Pieterzoon Sweelinck (1562–1621), who was one of the principal musicians to develop organ music before German composer Johann Sebastian Bach.

The Netherlands has produced many talented musicians. The Royal Concertgebouw Orchestra in Amsterdam and the Residentie Orchestra in The Hague are two of the finest ensembles in the world. Dutch musicians also pioneered the use of period instruments in modern concerts. Today, the Amsterdam Baroque Orchestra and Orchestra of the Eighteenth Century are famous worldwide for giving such performances.

In some Dutch towns, music can be heard on the streets throughout the day. Street musicians perform with instruments ranging from the humble harmonica to traditional barrel organs and carillons. The ornately decorated barrel organ produces cheerful, rollicking sounds, while the carillon, with its fixed bells, produces gentle harmony.

Above: **Talented street musicians often perform in Amsterdam's Dam Square.**

AMSTERDAM

Once a humble fishing village, Amsterdam grew to become not only the capital of the Netherlands but also the country's cultural center.
(A Closer Look, page 44)

Architecture

During the Middle Ages, the period between the late fifth and mid-fourteenth centuries, the Gothic style of architecture was most popular in the Netherlands. Today, many Dutch towns still have a few Gothic buildings standing in their old areas. Although introduced later on, the Classical style of architecture never overtook the Gothic style. The Golden Age in the seventeenth century gave rise to impressive mansions and canal houses. Limited space in the urban areas led to the establishment of building laws, which restricted the size of houses to the width of three windows. Consequently, most houses of this period are narrow and tall. Also, apart from ornately decorated gables, these houses are usually rather plain.

Architects in the twentieth century worked especially hard after World War II. Not only did they have to restore the areas devastated by war, they also had to accommodate the swiftly expanding postwar urban population.

Above: **The most intriguing housing development in recent years is the cluster of tilted cube houses in Rotterdam. Designed by Piet Blom, the houses stand on tall columns, which, in turn, stand on a raised pedestrian walkway.**

WINDMILLS

The country's inventive architecture is not the only testament to Dutch innovation. The windmill came to be a Dutch icon not because the Dutch invented the windmill but because of their clever use of it.

(*A Closer Look*, page 70)

Furniture

Dutch furniture is generally solid and intricately detailed but hardly ever flamboyant. Dutch furniture-makers reached an artistic peak in the sixteenth century. Some of the most impressive wardrobes, for example, were made during the Renaissance. Significantly large, each wardrobe had four doors and a cornice on top. They also featured intricate carvings of lions, scrolls, and various geometric patterns.

Lacquered furniture was popular among the sailors who traveled to the Far East in the days of the Dutch East India Company, and it is still favored by the locals on the Wadden Islands. Many houses also contain big Frisian clocks, cherished by the Dutch since the invention of the pendulum by Dutchman Christian Huygens in the seventeenth century.

DELFT PORCELAIN

Authentic delftware *(above)* is marked with the letter "D" and is one of the finest types of porcelain in the world. *(A Closer Look, page 48)*

Traditional Crafts

People in villages and small towns have kept their traditional crafts alive. Pottery is produced throughout the country, but the most well-known ceramics are made in Delft. Wooden shoes are worn by farmers on a daily basis. These shoes, however, are not the same as those mass-produced and sold as souvenirs. In southern Netherlands, the women make beautiful lace, which is usually sewn onto traditional Dutch costumes.

Left: These wooden shoes are not worn by locals. They are sold, instead, to tourists as souvenirs.

33

Leisure and Festivals

Hobbies

Most Dutch people spend their free time at home with their families. A popular home-based hobby is gardening. Many working people spend their weekends in their gardens, tidying up the flower beds and looking after their plants. In fact, gardening is so popular that families living in apartments even rent little allotments on the outskirts of town so they can cultivate flowers and some vegetables.

In the evening, nothing beats a cozy chat at home by the fireside, especially in the winter when the weather is damp and cold. Reading the newspaper or a good book with a warm drink nearby is also part of the Dutch vision of cozy home life, and musically inclined families often listen to their favorite albums or even make some music of their own.

Left: **This man in Amsterdam is making sure his treasured plants have everything they need.**

Café Culture

The café lifestyle is firmly entrenched in Dutch society. Dutch cafés come in two main types: the "brown" and the "white" cafés. A visit to a brown café is popular with the older generation. Full of character, the cafés are called brown because their walls are stained with tobacco smoke, which has filled these cafés for years. Furnished with comfortable chairs and tables with thick tablecloths, they look more like homey living rooms than coffeehouses. Patrons usually order a drink that is often served with cheese or peanuts. Brown cafés also feature a large table covered with books and magazines and allow patrons to stay as long as they like.

White cafés, on the other hand, try to be as different from their brown counterparts as possible. They are modernist in design, with lots of open space and light. White and brown cafés offer similar menu options, although white cafés provide a wider variety of gourmet coffee and cakes. White cafés also tend to cater to a younger, more urban crowd. While these establishments try to keep the premises white, smoking is allowed.

Soccer

The Dutch are huge soccer fans, and almost every male has played the game at least once in his life. In addition to playing the game, thousands of devoted fans show up at the stadiums to watch soccer matches. Entire families often attend matches that feature their favorite teams. The more popular clubs include Ajax Amsterdam, Feyenoord Rotterdam, and PSV Eindhoven. These teams are among the best in European soccer. In the 1970s, the Dutch national soccer team was considered one of the best in the world, although they have yet to win the much-coveted World Cup. Led by the legendary Johan Cruyff, the team twice came

close to becoming world champions (1974 and 1978) but was beaten in the finals both times. Today, many Dutch professional soccer players play for some of the best clubs in other countries.

Euro 2000

For twenty-three days in the summer of 2000, Belgium and the Netherlands hosted one of the biggest sporting events in Europe — the Euro 2000 soccer championships. Sixteen of the best European national teams competed against one another. The opening game took place in Belgium, but the finals were played in Rotterdam. Throughout the event, teams and supporters alike shuttled between the two countries, and star players from different teams wowed the crowds with their skills.

Above: **Soccer fever gripped the country in the summer of 2000, when some of the Euro 2000 games were played in the Netherlands. Dutch men, women, and children turned up in force to support their national team.**

Other Sports

The very flat terrain of the Netherlands is ideal for cycling and walking. Dutch cyclists regularly take part in the Tour de France, the most prestigious cycling event in the world, while competitive walkers take part in the four-day Nijmegen marathon, a grueling test of endurance.

Water sports are also very popular because there are so many lakes and canals throughout the country. In summer, swimming, sailing, and water-skiing draw many people to the beaches and lakes. Frozen lakes and canals in winter become temporary skating rinks for adults and children alike. The *Elfstedentocht* (elf-STAY-den-tokt), or "Eleven Towns Race," in Friesland is a marathon skating competition covering a distance of 125 miles (200 km) passing through eleven towns. This race, which attracts thousands of participants, can be held only during very cold winters, when all the canals are frozen.

TRADITIONAL SPORTS

The Dutch people enjoy some very unusual traditional sports. In Friesland, *fierljeppen* (feerl-YEP-pen) involves vaulting over canals or ditches with the help of a long pole. Frisians are also very enthusiastic about *wadlopen* (vad-LOH-pun), which involves walking on the mud flats uncovered by receding tides. In southwestern Netherlands, a five-day pole-sitting marathon takes place every year. The person who can remain on the pole for the longest time wins.

Left: Wind-surfing is one of the many types of water sports the Dutch enjoy in the warmer months.

Carnival

Carnival is celebrated in all parts of the Netherlands, but the more lavish celebrations take place in the south. In Maastricht, for example, preparations for Carnival start as early as mid-November each year, even though the festival is in February or March, forty days before Easter.

About three weeks before the festival, shop owners decorate their windows, and brass bands begin to stage regular performances at local nightspots as well as at children's clubs. A few days before Carnival weekend, young men accompany women who roam the streets dressed as witches or old hags. At the stroke of midnight, the women remove their masks and receive kisses from the men. On the Monday before the festival, children wear fancy clothes and search every part of town for the Carnival Prince, a costumed figure.

Carnival Day is celebrated with numerous processions featuring grotesque giant puppets and colorful floats. Masked revelers, both young and old, walk through the streets playing musical instruments and singing. At the festival's end, everyone sings a song together, which marks, at the same time, the beginning of the solemn period of Lent.

Queensday

The Dutch people celebrate Queensday, which is officially the queen's birthday, on April 30 every year. Although Queen Beatrix was born in February, she decided to keep Queensday on April 30, which is the birthday of the former queen, her mother, because the weather is better in April than in February. Queensday is a public holiday and one of the most important national celebrations of the year.

As part of the Queensday celebrations, the queen visits a different town every year. She wears either a traditional Dutch costume or something orange, which is the queen's color because she descended from the House of Orange. The lucky residents of the town the queen visits pack the streets to get a glimpse of her. Street artists, such as musicians, acrobats, and magicians, perform for the pedestrians, while people elsewhere convert the entire country into a giant flea market. Queensday is the only day of the year when Dutch citizens are allowed to sell anything they wish wherever they like without first obtaining licenses.

SINTERKLAAS

The Dutch always celebrate Christmas, or *Sinterklaas* (SIN-ter-klahs), with their families. Children receive candy as well as toys during Sinterklaas on December 6, while adults receive their presents on Christmas Day, when the family gets together for a feast of roast turkey.

(*A Closer Look, page 64*)

Opposite: **Carnival celebrations always draw lavishly costumed people.**

Below: **Held in summer, the Flower Festival in Aalsmeer features a procession of floats decorated with flowers.**

Food

Dutch food is reputed to be heavy and bland, relying on the natural flavors of meats and animal fat. For centuries, Dutch cooks have prepared simple and hearty meals using meat or fish and vegetables. Such high-calorie dishes were once a necessity in a country with icy winters and damp weather. Today, however, the people lead a much more sedentary lifestyle, and Dutch cuisine is becoming lighter. Many cooks omit lard and animal fats from traditional dishes and include more vegetables and fruit. More and more people are also becoming vegetarians.

Regional Specialties

Each province has a special dish made from local products. Northerners are heavy meat eaters because most keep their own chickens, cattle, and pigs. In Zeeland, the specialty is seafood, such as mussels, oysters, sole, and turbot. Many restaurants in the region are built on stilts at the water's edge. Stews and soups are popular in many provinces. In Maastricht, Limburg, the local dish is a stew resembling Hungarian goulash.

HISTORY OF HOTPOT STEW

In Leiden, the hotpot stew comes with a story. Made every October 3, the hotpot stew commemorates the town's liberation from the Spanish in 1574. The dish consists of boneless beef ribs, carrots, potatoes, and onions.

Below: **The Dutch enjoy most meat and vegetable dishes.**

Left: Seafood is a favorite among the Dutch people who live along the southwestern coast of the Netherlands.

Traditional Favorites

Thick soups and mashed vegetable dishes are firm favorites with the Dutch, especially with the older generation. The most traditional winter dish is cabbage mashed with potatoes and served with smoked sausage. Other types of vegetables are also mashed and flavored with bacon fat. The most popular soup is green-pea soup.

Herring is also a traditional favorite. In May, when the first herring of the season are caught, wooden stands spring up throughout the country to sell this delicacy. The fish is usually eaten as a snack and can be served either raw or cooked. When eaten raw, herring is held by the tail and put whole into the mouth. When cooked, the fish is served on a small plate and topped with plenty of chopped onions.

Pancakes and waffles are popular desserts, and, whether eaten at home or on the streets, they are always doused in syrup, even if the filling is salty. *Boterletter* (boh-ter-LET-ter) is puff pastry with a melt-in-the-mouth almond filling. It is eaten during Sinterklaas.

The country's most popular drink at any time of the day is coffee, dark and strong for adults and with a splash of chocolate milk, which can be either hot or cold, for children.

RIJSTAFFEL

The Indonesian *rijstaffel* (RICE-tah-fel) has become a fixture of Dutch cuisine. Rijstaffel, which means "rice table," is a meal of rice accompanied by an array of up to thirty dishes. Regular dishes in a rijstaffel include *sate* (SAH-teh), which are grilled skewers of meat served with a peanut sauce; egg curry; shrimp in a spicy sauce; and pieces of roast pork. The dishes are eaten with a fork in the left hand and a spoon in the right hand.

A CLOSER LOOK AT THE NETHERLANDS

Windmills, cheese, and tulips are images most commonly associated with the Netherlands. While the Dutch people keep these icons close to their hearts, they are especially proud of their welfare services, one of the most comprehensive in the world, and their feats of engineering, such as the Delta Project, which has saved large tracts of land from flooding. Amsterdam is the most well-known city in the country, not just for its physical beauty, but also for its architectural grandeur and culture, while the Wadden Islands are comparatively primitive and remote.

Opposite: **With many varieties of flowers in full bloom, the Netherlands is breathtakingly beautiful in spring.**

The Dutch people have produced some of the greatest thinkers in the world, such as Erasmus, the theologian, and Grotius, the jurist. Rembrandt is not only the finest painter to emerge from seventeenth-century Netherlands but also one of the greatest artists of all time. Among Dutch women, two diametrically opposed figures stand out. Mata Hari, the notorious seductress of the early twentieth century, was executed for treason during World War I, while Anne Frank spent much of her short life hiding from the Nazis in Amsterdam. The Dutch have a zest for life that they display during quaint celebrations, such as Sinterklaas. They also have great affection for their queen and pride for their regional costumes.

Above: **The Europoort is one of the busiest ports in the world. It handles most of the goods that are headed for other countries in the European Union.**

Amsterdam

A Humble Beginning

The city of Amsterdam began as a small fishing village near a dam that was built on the River Amstel in the thirteenth century. Initially called Amstelredam, which means "dam on the Amstel," the village quickly blossomed into an important trade center.

From the sky, Amsterdam looks like a spider web, with canals going around it and roads linking the canals. A river, the Singel, and three main canals flow around the city center. The Singel was originally part of a moat that protected the city. The three canals were constructed during a period of great expansion in the seventeenth century, during the Netherlands' Golden Age. Areas around the Herengracht (Gentlemen's Canal), Keizersgracht (Emperor's Canal), and Prinsengracht (Prince's Canal) were reserved for the homes and offices of the rich and more powerful city merchants, while citizens of lesser means lived near one of the outer canals.

Below: **Built along canals, Amsterdam is a beautiful and romantic city.**

Building Character and Identity

The Herengracht, in particular, is lined with many grand buildings. These structures were built according to a set of architectural guidelines, producing a sense of uniformity broken only by ornately decorative gables. As taxes were levied according to the width of the property, most buildings tended to be tall and narrow. In the past, long wooden beams were commonly seen protruding from the attics of these houses. These fixtures were used to hoist furnishings and other merchandise from the street up to the top floors. Many buildings tilt slightly toward the pavement so that rainwater flowing off the roofs drips onto the street without coming into contact with the buildings' facades.

Museums

Some of the most popular places in Amsterdam are the art museums. The largest is the Rijksmuseum, where a vast collection of art appears to have drawn much of its inspiration from the city itself. Containing some of the best seventeenth-century Dutch paintings in the world, the museum also displays rare pieces of medieval and Asian art. Other museums of art are the Van Gogh Museum and the Stedelijk, which specializes in modern art.

A PERMISSIVE CULTURE

Amsterdam is notorious for its liberal attitude toward prostitutes and drugs. The utilitarian motives behind such an attitude, however, are often mis- or unrepresented.

Prostitutes are seen as victims in the eyes of Dutch law, and the legalization of prostitution was not a move to encourage the industry but to protect those who are already in it. Under this system, prostitutes are registered and go for regular health checks, keeping the spread of diseases, such as AIDS, under control.

Drugs are technically illegal in the Netherlands, but Dutch authorities tend to ignore mild substances for personal use. The government concentrates on tackling the far more serious problem of hard drugs.

Cheeses of the Netherlands

Dutch cheeses enjoy a good reputation throughout the world, but they taste a whole lot better at home than overseas. The Dutch keep the better quality cheeses for themselves and export only what they do not consume. The two most famous Dutch cheeses are Gouda, which is customarily molded into large, round disks, and Edam, which looks more like a ball. Edam cheese is made mainly for export and is not readily available in the country. Both Edam and Gouda are made from cow's milk.

OTHER TYPES OF DUTCH CHEESES

Dutch cheeses include Leidse, which is Gouda with cumin seeds; Leerdammer and Maasdammer, which are strong in flavor and full of holes; Emmental; and Gruyére.

Left: Alkmaar comes alive with a traditional cheese market every year.

The Netherlands produces six major types of cheeses. Many Dutch cheeses are variations of the hard, mild Gouda, with differences resulting from their age. Young cheese has a mild flavor, while cheese that has matured for at least four months is much tastier. Old cheese can be pungent and flaky, much like Parmesan cheese. The Dutch enjoy their cheese in thin slices rather than in big chunks. Cheese is also a very popular sandwich filling.

Today, cheese is sold directly from the producer to the wholesaler. Cheese-producing towns, such as Edam, Gouda, and Alkmaar, however, still retain their traditional cheese markets because of the lucrative tourist industry. In the past, the disks of cheese were piled high onto a wooden sled and carried by porters to the weighing house to be weighed, as well as assessed for texture and taste. The porters were always dressed in white shirts and trousers, and they also wore leather slings, which had pieces of rope at the lower ends that the porters tied to one end of the sled. Two porters, one at either end of the sled, often carried more than ten disks of cheese at a time.

In the weighing house, details of the assessment were marked on the cheese and formed the basis for the price negotiation between buyers and sellers. When a mutually acceptable price was reached, both parties would clap their hands to signify the closing of the deal.

DUTCH CHEESE SOUP

The Dutch love to eat cheese so much that they even have a recipe for cheese soup. Potatoes, carrots, celery sticks, and cauliflower are cut into bite-size pieces and boiled in chicken broth. Thin slices of Gouda cheese and bacon are then added to the soup, which is commonly eaten with toast.

Delft Porcelain

Dutch potters began to produce majolica, a type of tin-glazed pottery, in the sixteenth century. Majolica was named after the Mediterranean island of Majorca, where the technique of producing such pottery originated. Over time, many Dutch makers of majolica gathered in the towns of Delft and Haarlem, where they made mainly wall tiles for kitchens. These tiles proved to be very popular with Dutch housewives because they kept out dust and dampness. Originally inspired by Moorish or Spanish patterns, the tiles began to appear more Dutch in design, with the inclusion of ships, flowers, animals, and children at play.

Delft did not become a center for fine porcelain until the early seventeenth century, when the local potters began to imitate the delicate blue and white porcelain brought in from China by the Dutch East India Company. Consequently, the demand for majolica, which was much coarser in comparison, suffered a sharp decline, and many pottery houses went bankrupt. Those

Below: **The makers of traditional delft porcelain also make products with a more modern appeal.**

Left: Traditional Delft porcelain is painstakingly crafted.

still in business turned to making blue and white ware, with designs that were modeled after Chinese pottery. In 1645, however, civil war broke out in China, which caused a major drop in the supply of imported porcelain, and demand for delftware boomed. At first, Dutch potters continued to produce only tiles, plates, and panels, but by the mid-seventeenth century, they had begun to make jars, vases, and ornamental wall pieces. Motifs also changed to reflect the origin of the ceramics, with painters drawing scenes from Dutch life and landscapes.

The Dutch pottery industry suffered a major blow in the mid-eighteenth century, when less expensive, mass-produced English ceramics flooded the market. By the mid-nineteenth century, only the Koninklijke Porceleyne Fles factory was still in business in Delft. Since then, delftware has become synonymous with the finest porcelain. Today, many museums in the Netherlands, as well as people all over the world, are proud of their valuable collections produced by the early Delft potters.

THE KONINKLIJKE PORCELEYNE FLES FACTORY

The Koninklijke Porccleyne Fles factory in Delft has been crafting high-quality blue and white delftware since 1653. For a small fee, visitors are allowed to tour the factory premises. Inside, artisans demonstrate their painting skills, and a multimedia presentation illustrates the history and production of the porcelain. One of the factory's most remarkable projects is the tiled interior of the restaurant at the Hotel Port van Cleve in Amsterdam.

The Delta Project

One of the greatest feats of Dutch engineering was the Delta Project, so-called because it was situated at the delta where five major rivers — Rhine, Maas, IJssel, Waal, and Schelde — empty into the North Sea. The region had always been prone to severe flooding, the worst of which occurred in February 1953. This disaster drowned nearly 2,000 people, destroyed 47,000 homes, and ruined 718 square miles (1,860 square km) of fertile farmland. In 1957, the Dutch government launched the Delta Project, an ambitious plan to seal off 430 miles (692 km) of tidal flats and flood-prone estuaries. The bulk of the project, which cost 6.5 billion guilders (U.S. $15.6 billion), took twenty-nine years (1957–1986) to complete.

In a move that aimed to protect as much land as quickly as possible, as well as allow the engineers to learn as they went along, the smaller, secondary dams were built first. Even these smaller dams, however, led to unforeseen problems. The short stretch of dam at Haringvliet, for example, turned out to require sixty-five massive pilings, each 175 feet (53 m) deep.

THE DELTA EXPO

The Delta Expo is a permanent exhibition to explain the reclamation project. Located on one of the artificial islands of the Storm Surge Barrier, the exhibition explains the local ecology as well as the project's effects on fish farming. Boat visits to the computer-controlled sluice gates give visitors an idea of the scale of the project.

Below: Completed in 1970, this section of the Delta Project, in southwestern Netherlands, is called the Haringvliet Dam.

The greatest stumbling block, however, arose in 1968, when work began on the largest dam, which was designed to close the East Schelde estuary. Environmentalists and local fishermen objected to the project, warning against the resulting loss of valuable breeding grounds for birds and fish. If the estuary was closed, the oyster, mussel, and lobster beds would be destroyed, and thousands of fishermen would lose their livelihood. Finally, a compromise was reached with the design of a supremely elegant and intelligent piece of engineering. Completed in 1986, the Storm Surge Barrier remains open under normal tidal conditions, allowing free flow of water between the North Sea and the estuary, but slams shut in times of unusually high tides, which occur about once every eighteen months. Made up of sixty-two enormous gates, the barrier permits 85 percent of natural tidal movement. To build the barrier, two artificial islands were created in the estuary.

The Delta Project not only saved the farmlands of Zeeland, but it was also a draw for tourism in the area. The dams gave rise to highways between the islands in the delta and helped link the Randstad to the southwestern part of the Netherlands.

Above: **The Philips Dam was completed in 1987 and has a special system that separates salt water from freshwater.**

Dutch Thinkers

Erasmus (1466–1536)

Born in Rotterdam on October 27, Desiderius Erasmus Roterodamus received the best education a young man of his time could get. After graduating from a series of monastic or semi-monastic schools, he was admitted to the priesthood and took monastic vows in 1492. Yet he never practiced as a monk. Rather, he continued to study theology and spent the rest of his life reflecting and writing on the doctrine and institutions of Christianity. Although he was offered positions in various academic institutions throughout Europe, Erasmus declined them all, preferring to pursue his independent literary activity.

Grotius (1583–1645)

A child prodigy, Hugo Grotius (Huig de Groot) was born in Delft and received his doctorate in law at the age of fifteen. Otherwise known as "the father of international law," Grotius wrote extensively about the laws of war and peace. He did not believe

Left: Erasmus thought of himself as, above all else, a preacher of righteousness. He was critical of the formalism in the Catholic Church and believed that what Europe needed to regenerate itself was sound learning that was applied frankly and fearlessly to the administration of public life in Church and State. Erasmus, however, remained neutral throughout the Reformation resistance led by the Protestants. *Praise of Folly* (1509) remains the most well-known of his works, and he was responsible for the new edition and Latin translation of the New Testament.

that a person's destiny was preordained by God, which was the dominant belief in the culture at that time. He believed people could choose their destinies, and he was jailed in 1619 for maintaining the stance. Two years later, he broke out of jail and escaped to Paris. In the later part of his life, he became a lawyer and a diplomat. A pioneering scholar of the law, Grotius was possibly the first person to view the world as a global community.

Above, left: **Grotius started composing Latin verses at the age of eight and attended university when he was eleven years old.**

Above, right: **The work of Spinoza is still widely cited in universities worldwide today.**

Spinoza (1632–1677)

Baruch Spinoza was born into a Jewish family that had fled to Amsterdam from persecution in Portugal. Trained in Talmudic scholarship, he engaged in a profound study of medieval Jewish thought as well as modern philosophy and science. Expelled from the Amsterdam synagogue for his heretical views in 1656, he supported himself by grinding optical lenses, refusing all honors and giving his share of his father's inheritance to his sister. He died of tuberculosis in 1677, probably aggravated by the fine glass dust inhaled at the workbench. In all his writings, Spinoza encouraged readers to strive for peace of mind by acknowledging the limits of logic and reason.

Flowers of the Netherlands

The Dutch love affair with flowers dates back to the late sixteenth century, when botanist Carolus Clusius brought the first tulip bulb to the Netherlands from Turkey. As the flowers bloomed in the sandy Dutch soil, growers began to view the tulip as a gold mine. In the 1630s, a period remembered as "Tulipomania," demand for the flowers was so high in all of northern Europe that investors traded in the bulbs on a purely speculative basis. The rarest bulbs often fetched prices that were more than two thousand times the weekly wage of the average worker. The bulbs traveled easily, and the rare and colorful flowers were a popular way to flaunt one's wealth. The most popular tulips at that time were of the multicolored, or striated, variety. By the time reality set in in 1637, many victims of "Tulipomania" had lost their entire fortunes.

Below: **Public parks and gardens in the Netherlands become breathtakingly beautiful in spring.**

Today, in addition to tulips, about ten thousand Dutch growers also cultivate roses, carnations, and an assortment of bulbous plants, which include crocuses, daffodils, narcissi, gladioli, and hyacinths. The Dutch flower industry, which is centered in Leiden in Zuid-Holland, is one of the country's main industries and helps the tourist industry by attracting millions of visitors to the blooming fields and flower exhibitions every year. Dutch bulb fields cover more than 65 square miles (168 square km) of the country's land and produce 65 percent of the world's supply, which is about 9 billion bulbs a year. The tulip, however, is only the country's fourth best-selling flower, behind roses, chrysanthemums, and carnations.

Flowers and Tourism

In spring, Dutch fields become a riot of colors, and the tourist information centers even set up "flower routes" to guide visitors. The Keukenhof Gardens, which are halfway between Leiden and Haarlem, are the largest in the world. Over 6 million flowers, spread over almost 338,800 square yards (283,237 square m), are on display every year throughout their flowering period. The largest flower auction takes place in Aalsmeer, which is northeast of Leiden. Visitors can witness the fast and furious dealing, which amounts to an average of about 800 million guilders (U.S. $336 million) worth of flowers and plants traded in one year.

FOREIGN LABOR

Most of the workers who pack and label bulbs are migrant laborers. They work sixteen-hour shifts for wages no Dutch person would even consider. They arrive at work at 7:30 a.m. and toil until late in the evening, packing and labeling tulip and hyacinth bulbs. In addition to the long working hours, they also have to put up with the health hazards posed by handling the bulbs. Dust from the bulbs, for example, causes the workers' fingers to swell or become infected, leading to a condition known as "bulb finger." Although the workers are provided with coats and gloves, the heat in the warehouses makes wearing them unbearable.

Mata Hari

Margarethe Geertruide Zelle was born in 1876 in Leeuwarden, Friesland. She was to become the notorious Mata Hari, a name synonymous with the term *femme fatale* today. Margarethe married Campbell MacLeod, a British-born captain in the Dutch army, after completing her education in a convent. She was eighteen at that time. MacLeod was stationed in the Dutch East Indies, so she moved with him to East Java, where she had two children. While in Java, she learned, among other things, the phrase *mata hari*, which means "eye of the dawn" in Indonesian, and Javanese dancing. The couple, however, left the island hurriedly after their son was killed. Upon returning to the Netherlands, MacLeod descended into alcoholism. Margarethe was consequently granted a divorce, and she headed for Paris in 1900, after leaving her daughter with relatives.

Left: **In 1932, Mata Hari's story was brought to the big screen in a movie starring Greta Garbo *(left)* as the famous spy. The film became one of Garbo's greatest successes at the box office. Despite her notoriety, Mata Hari's childhood home in Leeuwarden now houses the Frisian Literary Museum.**

With no money and no skills, Margarethe assumed the invented identity of Mata Hari, the daughter of a Hindu Brahmin who had supposedly imparted to her the initiation rites and rituals of the Kandaswami sacred dance. Mata Hari's early audiences were guests at private parties, but she soon went on to perform for the affluent soldiers and statesmen who visited the Folies Bergères, the most famous music hall in Paris. Her dances were so popular, in fact, that she became an international star.

When Margarethe arrived in The Hague in 1915, she abandoned the identity of Mata Hari, taking on, instead, the persona of a wealthy woman. She also assumed various nationalities, including German. During these years, and especially during World War I, she had close connections with many men, including high-ranking officers from both the German and Allied sides. Although no hard evidence of spy activity was ever found, she was arrested by French intelligence, charged with spying, imprisoned, and ultimately executed.

CONVICTED ON QUESTIONABLE EVIDENCE

During Mata Hari's trial, the only piece of "evidence" that was used to convict her was that she reportedly attended a school for espionage in Lorrach, Germany, in 1907 and had been given a secret German spy number — H12.

Mata Hari was executed in front of a large crowd in Paris on October 15, 1917. She refused to be bound or blindfolded, and she blew a kiss to the firing squad before they pulled their triggers.

The Monarchy

The House of Orange

Unlike its English counterpart, the House of Windsor, the Dutch House of Orange attracts very little media attention. The lifestyle of the Dutch royal family is decidedly low-key and almost ordinary. The Dutch monarch, Queen Beatrix, is affectionately called "monarch on a bicycle," because of her preference for this humble mode of transportation. The royal family's sense of modesty endears them to the Dutch people, who are fiercely egalitarian. A showy and extravagant ruler would not be admired or tolerated.

Although the House of Orange has a history that dates back to the Middle Ages, the family became royalty only in the late sixteenth century, after playing a prominent part in securing the country's independence. Playing a unifying role and proclaiming a high moral stance, the House of Orange earned the respect of the people and went on to lead the country to great prosperity.

FAMILY MOTTO

The family motto of the House of Orange is a French phrase — *Je maintiendrai*, which means "I shall maintain." The family has, indeed, lived up to the motto, maintaining a dignified and antimilitarist stance that has found great favor with the Dutch people.

Left: **A dedicated freedom fighter, William I of Orange is honored by the Dutch as a national hero for founding a tradition of democracy and egalitarianism.**

Queen Beatrix

Although Queen Beatrix is the second-richest woman in the world, with an estimated fortune of 5 billion guilders (U.S. $2 billion), neither she nor the rest of her family make ostentatious displays of wealth. Instead of being chauffeured around in luxury cars, she rides her bicycle and has a preference for local foods rather than expensive imported wines and food. She has a deep respect for the common people, and she sees her role in the country as a means to better the lives of everyone. If she had not been queen, she once said, she would have become a social worker.

Despite having strong support for their royal family, the Dutch people can be quite critical of their rulers. The 1966 wedding of then-Princess Beatrix to Claus von Amsberg, a German diplomat who was a former member of the Hitler Youth and the Wehrmacht, or the German army, caused violent demonstrations throughout the country. The Dutch people will never forget the horrors of the German occupation and saw the marriage as an insult to their sensitivities. Prince Claus, however, has managed to steer clear of any controversy and has become a well-respected member of the royal family.

Above: **The Dutch royal family is always careful not to inflate its role in public life. Because the family maintains such a low profile, the Dutch people, in turn, respect the family's privacy.**

EDUCATING BEATRIX
Queen Beatrix spent the first seven years of her life in the United Kingdom, before returning to the Netherlands to attend public schools in Baarn, where she was born. She went on to pursue a law degree at Leiden University.

Regional Costumes

In the Netherlands, traditional costumes vary slightly from region to region but the main features are similar. Women wear tight-fitting jackets and long, loose skirts, which are usually dark in color and sometimes pleated. Striped or multi-colored aprons are worn over these skirts. Dutch women also wear peaked or winged caps, which are frequently made of lace. White caps are usually worn on Sundays, and they are positioned over the weekday cap, which is often black in color.

Men wear double-breasted jackets with long, baggy trousers that have silver buckles and buttons. Although the jacket and the trousers are usually black, the shirt is often

Below: **In the rural areas, both adults and children wear their regional costumes on many occasions. In the cities, however, young people sometimes tend to be more self-conscious of wearing native dress.**

bright in color or striped. The shirt is distinctive because it has a straight collar and is fastened with gold buttons. Men also wear hats, which are either dark, beret-like caps tied at either side or straw boaters in white or bright colors.

Variations are usually more apparent in women's clothing. However, in Marken, an island about 17 miles (27 km) northeast of Amsterdam, menswear differs from the standard apparel and consists of a red sash and a blue smock over baggy trousers. In some parts of Flevoland, women wear a distinctive light-blue plastron, which is a piece of square, embroidered cloth designed to be pinned on the shoulders. The men in that region wear shorter trousers to reveal intricately knitted stockings. In the conservative towns of Staphorst and Rouveen in Overijssel, the women's clothes are most often a dull, dark blue.

Wooden Shoes

One traditional item that is worn widely is wooden shoes. Unlike the pointy-toed clogs manufactured for the souvenir market, wooden shoes are shaped like most other shoes and may not look like wood because they are often painted black.

Rembrandt

Rembrandt Harmenszoon van Rijn was born in Leiden in 1606. At the age of fourteen, his family sent him to Leiden University to study theology, which did not interest him. He opted, instead, to study art under the supervision of Jacob van Swanenburch, a specialist in scenes of hell. A few years later, the young artist moved to Amsterdam and studied under Pieter Lastman (1583–1633), a famous historical painter. In 1624, Rembrandt returned to Leiden to set up a studio. He swiftly developed a reputation as a fine portraitist and painter of historical scenes. The man was so talented that he took his first student at the age of twenty-two.

In 1631, Rembrandt returned to Amsterdam to further his career. In 1634, he married Saskia van Uylenburgh, the niece of a noted art dealer, and this relationship brought him many wealthy patrons who commissioned him to paint their portraits. Rembrandt and Saskia had four children, of whom only the youngest survived to adulthood. In 1639, at the height of his career, Rembrandt borrowed heavily to buy a beautiful house. His debts mounted over time, and he had to declare bankruptcy

Left: **The Dutch erected this memorial to honor Rembrandt, one of the most famous painters the Netherlands has ever produced.**

Left: **This Rembrandt painting, titled *The Artist's Father*, is part of the collection at the Art Institute of Chicago.**

in 1666. The artist never recovered from this financial debacle and died a poor man in 1669.

Rembrandt was a master of chiaroscuro, which is the juxtapositioning of light and shadows for dramatic effect. He specialized in portraits, as well as historical and Biblical scenes. His most famous painting, *Nightwatch* (1642), is a vividly colored tableau of guards preparing to take up their stations. It is now displayed in Amsterdam's Rijksmuseum. The series of self-portraits the artist did during his lifetime are also of great artistic value. Rembrandt also produced numerous drawings and etchings, several of which are works of art in themselves.

Although Rembrandt was a prolific painter, sometimes completing one painting a month, many experts believe he did not paint all six hundred paintings attributed to him. Art experts today are still trying to identify the artist or artists who produced many of the paintings attributed to Rembrandt.

OTHER PAINTINGS BY REMBRANDT

Rembrandt's celebrated works include *St. Paul in Prison* (1627), *Supper at Emmaus* (1630), *The Anatomy Lesson of Doctor Nicolaes Tulp* (1632), *Young Girl at an Open Half-Door* (1645), *The Mill* (1650), and *Aristotle Contemplating the Bust of Homer* (1653).

Sinterklaas

The most popular festival among children in the Netherlands is Sinterklaas, which is celebrated from mid-November through the evening of December 5; it is the Dutch equivalent of Christmas. Sinterklaas is the Dutch name for Saint Nicholas, the patron saint of sailors and of the city of Amsterdam. Saint Nicholas was a bishop who lived in Turkey in the third and fourth centuries. According to legend, he did many good deeds, including saving his town from starvation and reviving three dead children. He also offered dowries to poor girls so they could get married.

In the Netherlands, Sinterklaas arrives on a steamboat from Spain in mid-November every year. He is an old man with white hair and a long white beard. He wears a bishop's headdress and a red cape and carries a long metal staff. Sinterklaas is always accompanied by a group of helpers called *Zwarte Piet* (zwar-tah PEET), meaning "Black Peter" because they are Moorish and dark-skinned. The Black Peters wear clothes typical of the seventeenth century: velvet jackets, caps with colored feathers, and starched white collars. After descending from the boat, Sinterklaas mounts a white horse and starts to parade throughout the Netherlands, handing out sweets and presents to good children. Those who have not been good are given a rod or are threatened with being carried away by the Black Peters in the big bag they always bring with them.

Sinterklaas leaves the Netherlands for Spain on December 6, the feast day of Saint Nicholas. The night before, children put carrots and hay in their shoes and place them in front of the chimney. In the course of the night, Sinterklaas lands on the roof and a Black Peter comes down the chimney with presents for the children. He also takes away the carrots and hay for the horse. School starts a few hours late on December 6 so children have time to play with their new toys.

Adults often receive anonymously given presents, called *surprises* (sir-PREEZ-us), during Sinterklaas. Wrapped to look like something else, surprises are actually humorous gifts or practical jokes and are accompanied by poems. The poems, which must be read out loud, usually contain embarrassing information about the person receiving the gift.

Above: **Early Dutch settlers brought the festival of Sinterklaas along with them when they moved to North America in the seventeenth century. Over the years, Sinterklaas, or Saint Nicholas, evolved into Santa Claus, the jolly old man who comes at Christmas. The Dutch-American community, however, still celebrates the tradition of Sinterklaas on December 6.**

Opposite: **Sinterklaas, or Saint Nicholas, waves at the crowd in Potsdam, Germany, where a significant number of Dutch immigrants live.**

Wadden Islands

Also known as the West Frisian Islands, the five Wadden Islands are remnants of an ancient natural dike, or sea wall, that lay between the North Sea and lowland marshes. The marshland was gradually submerged as the polar ice caps melted, converting the region into the Wadden Sea. Four of the islands belong to the province of Friesland, while the southernmost island, Texel, is part of the province of Noord-Holland.

The largest island, Texel, is also the most easily accessible. Much of the island's land area was reclaimed from the sea. Today, the island has large expanses of farmland. Numerous beaches, sand dunes, and woodlands are found along its western coast, which attracts large numbers of visitors during the summer. Several bird sanctuaries and nature reserves also dot the island. The De Slufter nature reserve has an open connection to the sea that encourages the development of unique plants, including the famous sea lavender that gives the valley a lovely lilac tint in the

Below: **A large portion of the largest Wadden island, Texel, is used for farming.**

THE SMALLER ISLANDS — VLIELAND AND SCHIERMONNIKOOG

Vlieland lies to the northeast of Texel and is the least developed island. Cars are banned, and tourism is modest. The island, however, has several precious nature reserves and is home to many species of birds.

In the seventeenth century, Vlieland was an important part of the whaling industry. Many tombstones in the local graveyard are made of whales' jawbones.

The waters around the island are treacherous, and many ships have sunk in the vicinity. The most well-known was the *Lutine*, a bullion ship that went down in 1799.

The easternmost island, Schiermonnikoog, is the smallest and quietest. It contains half of all the plant species in Europe, especially some very rare varieties of orchids. The island once belonged to the monastery of Klaarkamp on the mainland, and its name means "island of the gray monks."

summer months. With approximately three hundred species of birds, including gulls, terns, ringed plovers, avocets, and spoonbills, living on the island, Texel is also one of the most important breeding grounds for birds in Europe.

Terschelling lies to the northeast of Vlieland and is the middle island. Historically, the harbor town in western Terschelling was a major center for ship supplies and repair. The locals were also renowned sailors and pilots. Many ship captains who needed help navigating the shifting sandbanks of the Wadden Sea sought the skills of these locals. William Barents, after whom the Barents Sea is named, is possibly the most famous Terschelling native. He launched several expeditions into the forbidding Arctic region. One of the most popular spots in Terschelling is De Boschplant, a nature reserve. Built in 1594 and the largest lighthouse in the Netherlands, the Brandaris is also located on the island.

Ameland is the most commercial island and is one of the country's major tourist spots. About three thousand people live on the island permanently, but the population swells to a staggering thirty-five thousand during summer.

Welfare Services

The Dutch people are protected by a wide network of welfare services. Very few are considered poor, and the government sees to the needs of almost everyone. Caring for others has its roots in the Netherlands' long-established egalitarian society and belief in religious freedom. In the old days, religious organizations or family trusts built houses for the poor and the elderly. The poor and hungry of the sixteenth and seventeenth centuries were provided with food and shelter by various public and charitable organizations. Today, the needy in the Netherlands receive various forms of help from the government.

The Netherlands maintains a high standard of living, as well as one of the world's most generous social programs. All Dutch citizens are entitled to receive universal health care, free education, unemployment benefits, housing allowances, child support, old-age benefits, and much more. Students are paid to continue their education, and thousands of jobs are constantly created to keep people employed.

Left: **The Dutch Ministry of Health, Welfare, and Sport is located in The Hague.**

Left: A woman looking for work receives assistance at the unemployment office, where she is filling out the appropriate forms.

The Dutch educational system is among the best in the world. In the Netherlands, several types of schools are housed in the same building so students can transfer from one school to the next, depending on their abilities. Since students are not allowed to leave school until they are sixteen, those students who do poorly in one school simply move to another, where standards are somewhat lower and special attention is available. Unemployed people receive income support as well as holiday allowances that allow them to lead an independent lifestyle.

Families benefit from the General Family Allowance, which helps them support their children up to the age of eighteen. National Assistance specifically helps lower-income families. Health benefits are covered by four national insurance programs and four employee insurance programs. Employers must pay the salaries of sick employees for up to one year while they receive treatment. Retirement benefits are also very high, and former Dutch public servants receive especially good benefits.

HIGH TAXES

The government relies on high taxes to secure the financial resources needed to provide the extensive welfare network enjoyed by the Dutch people. As much as two-thirds of government revenue is redistributed to the people. As a result, the Dutch are one of the most heavily taxed peoples in the world, with rates ranging from a minimum of about 37 percent to a maximum of 68 percent. The Dutch people, however, do not complain because they can see the benefits of the welfare state for their society. They believe it is better to provide a safety net than to deal with the economic and social problems brought about by a lack of social services. In the Netherlands, crime rates are low, slums are almost nonexistent, and most people are employed.

Windmills

The windmill is a simple device that converts wind into useful energy. Energy is derived from the force of the wind that blows against big sails extending from a shaft. The moving sails rotate the shaft, which may be connected to machinery that can mill grain, pump water, or generate electricity. Although windmills were not invented by the Dutch, they have come to represent the Netherlands as much as wooden clogs and tulips.

Utilizing wind power was a concept that had spread from England and France, and the first windmill in the Netherlands appeared in the twelfth century. The apparatus, however, took about four hundred years to gain popularity in the country. The conversion of the windmill into a pump in the sixteenth century enabled the country to reclaim much more land than was

NATIONAL WINDMILL DAY

The Dutch people celebrate National Windmill Day on the second Saturday of May every year to coincide with the blooming of tulips. On this day, all windmills in the country are open to the public.

Left: Like other windmills throughout the world, windmills in the Netherlands were first used to grind grain.

Left: **These ultramodern wind turbines have replaced windmills in Friesland.**

previously possible. Buckets fitted to a wheel turned by wind power were used to scoop up large amounts of water and, thus, drain wide areas of land.

An innovative move that led to a much more efficient use of the windmill was the invention of an upper track. This track allowed the structure holding the sails together to be rotated. Before then, the sails faced a fixed direction, and the productivity of the windmill depended on the direction of the wind. With sails that could be rotated to face whichever way the wind blew, water could be scooped out constantly and efficiently.

To reclaim land, low-lying areas were dammed and drainage ditches built. A series of windmills were then used to scoop the water from the ditches and pour it into a larger canal positioned several feet higher. In 1620, more than twenty windmills were used to turn the area around Amsterdam into arable land, or land suitable for farming.

Dutch landlords began investing heavily in windmills when they saw the windmills' potential for land reclamation, and, by the nineteenth century, they had built about nine thousand windmills. Tenant farmers who rented plots of the newly reclaimed land used the landlord's windmill to grind their harvested grains at a cost. The windmills thus paid for themselves rapidly.

WINDMILLS TODAY

Windmills still dot the Dutch landscape, but more as ornaments than for utility. The technology used to reclaim land today is beyond the scope of windmills, and the few working windmills have reverted to their initial function of grinding grain. One of the best places to view windmills in the Netherlands is near Kinderdijk, a village about 60 miles (97 km) south of Amsterdam. All nineteen windmills are put in operation every Saturday afternoon during the summer months, and visitors are allowed to enter at least one of them.

A Young Girl and Her Journal

Anne Frank was just like any other ordinary adolescent, living a carefree lifestyle until World War II broke out. Like other girls her age, she wanted to look pretty and had hopes of becoming an actress in Hollywood. Her father, Otto, was a wealthy Jewish spice trader, who brought his family over to Amsterdam from Germany in 1933. In 1940, however, Germany invaded the Netherlands, and by 1942, life had become very harsh for Dutch Jews. In July 1942, just after Anne turned thirteen, Otto decided that his whole family should go into hiding to avoid the daily persecution of Jews. His business partner, who was also Jewish, had similar plans. This was how the two men came to live in the unused attic of their warehouse with their respective families. For two years, the Franks and the Van Daans lived behind a door disguised as a bookcase.

THE ANNE FRANK HOUSE

The warehouse that once sheltered the Franks and the Van Daans has since been converted into the Anne Frank House, a museum that details life in the hideaway more than fifty years ago. Visitors can learn about a little girl's hopes and dreams alongside the atrocities of the Nazis. The Anne Frank Foundation, which runs the museum, has an extensive educational program that aims to combat anti-Semitism and racism. The organization is also active in promoting democratic principles and individual initiatives for human rights.

Left: This photograph of Anne Frank *(right)* and her sister Margot *(left)* was taken in 1932 in Germany.

Left: During her two years of hiding, Anne Frank kept a journal detailing the day-to-day lives of the occupants of the attic, including petty quarrels, birthday celebrations, and news about the advance of the Allies into the Netherlands. Anne also described her feelings as she grew into a young adult, as well as her hopes and dreams.

ANNE FRANK'S DIARY

Translated into fifty-four languages, *Anne Frank's Diary* has sold more than 13 million copies worldwide and is on the reading list of many schools around the world. Some claim the book was a source of inspiration for Nelson Mandela while he was imprisoned in South Africa. Many read it for a glimpse of life under Nazi occupation and in memory of a girl whose only sin was to have been born into a certain race.

In 1944, however, just when the Allies began scoring victories in northern Europe, the Franks were betrayed by a Dutch Nazi sympathizer. The Germans forced open the fake bookcase and arrested all the occupants in the attic. The families were deported to separate concentration camps. Some went to Auschwitz in southwestern Poland, while others were sent to Bergen-Belsen in northwestern Germany. One week before the end of the war, in 1945, Anne and her sister died of typhus in Belsen. Of the eight people in the attic, only Otto Frank survived. When the war was over, he published his daughter's precious journal.

RELATIONS WITH NORTH AMERICA

The friendship between the Netherlands and North America began when the United States was a newly established nation. The Netherlands was not only the second country, after France, to recognize the new United States in 1782, it was also the first country to have a U.S. embassy. Since then, the two countries have maintained active foreign policies with each other. In 1776, the earliest version of the U.S. flag, with thirteen red and white stripes, was saluted by a Dutch colony. The governor of St. Eustatius, in the Caribbean, fired his cannons to welcome the *Andrew Doria*, a small ship bearing the flag.

Opposite: **The Netherlands and the United States have maintained mutually productive trade and investment relations for centuries.**

Above: **U.S. products and their advertisements can be found throughout the Netherlands.**

The Dutch were among the first settlers in the American colonies, and many communities in the New York area bear Dutch names. Dutch-Americans have made their presence felt throughout U.S. history in politics, industry, and entertainment.

Relations between the Netherlands and North America were further strengthened during World War II. Many American and Canadian troops took part in the liberation of the Netherlands in 1945. After the war, the Netherlands received financial aid from the United States under the Marshall Plan, an economic policy designed to rebuild European countries devastated by war.

The Hudson Expedition

In 1608, the Dutch East India Company hired Englishman Henry Hudson, a famous explorer, to look for a northeast passage to Southeast Asia from Europe. Hudson's vessel, the *Half Moon*, was soon blocked by the icy conditions north of Norway. Hudson turned around and decided instead to look for a route across the Atlantic Ocean. On July 1, 1609, the *Half Moon* reached Newfoundland, Canada. Hudson continued sailing southward, stopping only at present-day North Carolina, where he turned around and came back to the mouth of what is now the Hudson River. Thinking the river could lead to the Pacific Ocean, Hudson sailed up the river, reaching Albany before he realized his mistake. Hudson claimed the areas he had explored for the Dutch.

Above: **Henry Hudson died in 1611, shortly after he discovered the Hudson River.**

The Pilgrim Fathers

Also in 1608, the Pilgrim Fathers, a group of English religious dissidents, or nonconformists, left their homeland to avoid being persecuted for their unorthodox views. They first moved to the Netherlands, the most tolerant country in Europe at that time. The group's leaders, however, wanted freedom from all established nations and encouraged the Pilgrims to start a new life in the American colonies. The Pilgrims reached Cape Cod, Massachusetts, in 1620.

Opposite: **New Amsterdam was established after Peter Minuit bought Manhattan Island from the Indians for a mere 60 guilders (U.S. $25).**

Below: **An artistic impression of Hudson's discovery of Newfoundland in 1609.**

New Netherland

Following Hudson's discoveries, many Dutch ships sailed to America to trade with the American Indians, who supplied fur. No Dutch settlements, however, were established there until 1615, when the owners of the New Netherland Company secured exclusive rights to trade in an area called New Netherland (present-day New York and New Jersey). In 1621, the Dutch West India Company absorbed the New Netherland Company, acquiring as well the latter's monopoly on trade. The first group of Dutch immigrants arrived in 1624. A second group came one year later, but, unlike the first group, they were dispersed throughout the region. In 1626, Governor Peter Minuit decided to centralize all the Dutch immigrants, relocating them on the island of Manhattan. The new settlement was called New Amsterdam; it is New York City today.

Although busy and cosmopolitan, New Netherland never developed as well as other settlements in New England, which consisted of present-day Connecticut, Maine, Massachusetts, New Hampshire, Rhode Island, and Vermont. In 1664, the English captured New Netherland, which was under the command of Governor Peter Stuyvesant at that time.

JOHN ADAMS

The first U.S. president to be closely linked with the Netherlands was John Adams, the second president of the United States and the first U.S. ambassador to the Netherlands. Adams laid the foundation for Dutch-American relations by signing the Treaty of Amity and Trust with the Dutch in 1782. At the same time, Adams secured a loan of 5 million guilders (U.S. $2 million) from Amsterdam merchants and bankers for his fledgling nation. Today, the John Adams Institute, located in Amsterdam, promotes cultural exchanges between the United States and the Netherlands.

Trade Relations with the United States

The relationship between the Netherlands and the United States
has been described as one between "old friends." Indeed, the
Dutch were among the first to establish trade and investment
links with the United States. In 1997, bilateral trade between the
two countries reached nearly $30 billion. The United States is the
largest foreign investor in the Netherlands and is the single most
important market for the Dutch outside of Europe. The Dutch
have been among the top ten buyers of U.S. exports for years
and are the third-largest investor in the United States.

Politically, the Netherlands and the United States have been
allies since World War II. In 1949, both countries joined the North
Atlantic Treaty Organization (NATO), and the Netherlands has
proved to be loyal to the United States both within NATO and in
international politics. During the Korean War, Dutch and U.S.
troops fought side by side, and the Dutch provided naval support
to the U.S.-led coalition of nations during the Persian Gulf War in
the early 1990s.

Above: In April 2000,
Unilever, a Dutch
conglomerate, bought
Vermont-based Ben
and Jerry's, an ice
cream producer known
for its support of
charities. Unilever has
sixty-six offices and
manufacturing sites
in the United States.

Dutch People in the United States

Although the Dutch people were among the first to settle in the United States, they did not form a distinct group until the mid-nineteenth century. In fact, Dutch immigration came almost to a standstill after the English took control of New Netherland in 1664, with the exception of a group of two hundred people who founded what is now Germantown, a city near Philadelphia, in 1683. Mostly Quaker Christians, these Dutch people were joined by many like-minded Germans in the eighteenth century. By the time the United States gained independence in 1776, the United States had already welcomed 100,000 Dutch immigrants.

Dutch immigration increased significantly in the 1840s. Religious conflicts in 1845 and 1846 as well as overpopulation in Europe at that time spurred scores of Dutch people to move to the United States — a land of opportunity and religious freedom. Many of these new immigrants tended to settle in the Black Lake region in Michigan, establishing the first successful Dutch settlement in the United States since the days of the West India Company. Dutch immigration continued until the region between Lake Michigan and Grand Rapids was almost entirely populated by Dutch settlers.

Today, aside from the New York area and Michigan, significant Dutch communities can be found in Iowa, Minnesota, the Dakotas, Montana, Washington, Utah, and California.

Left: **A windmill and a model wooden shoe reflect Dutch heritage in Oak Harbor, Washington. Washington State has a large Dutch-American community.**

Dutch-American Friendship Day and Heritage Day

Every year, 8 million Americans of Dutch descent celebrate two events to mark the good relations between the United States and the Netherlands. Dutch-American Friendship Day, on April 19, commemorates the first time John Adams was received by the States-General in The Hague, as U.S. ambassador to the Netherlands. Dutch-American Heritage Day, November 16, marks the day in 1776 when the Netherlands was the first foreign nation to recognize the U.S. flag. Both days are celebrated in a modest and dignified manner, with exhibitions on the Netherlands and the strong bonds between the two countries. For most Dutch-Americans, the events are opportunities to relive their heritage and take pride in the fact that their ancestors started and maintained a four-hundred-year tradition of goodwill in the United States.

Winterfest

The town of Holland in Michigan organizes a Dutch Winterfest every year from late November to the end of December. The festival begins in the evening with a lantern parade through Centennial Park, which is lavishly decorated with lights. Children not only get to see live reindeer, they also watch Sinterklaas riding into town on a white horse. Another highlight of the festival is the Dutch Christmas Market, which features imported Dutch foods and crafts. Holland, Michigan, also has a 275-year-old windmill and a clog factory, which uses traditional methods to make clogs.

The North Sea Jazz Festival

The extensive cultural exchange between the two countries is also apparent in the Netherlands. Since 1976, the city of The Hague has been hosting the North Sea Jazz Festival, one of the highlights of the European cultural season. For three days in July, more than one thousand musicians entertain seventy thousand jazz enthusiasts from all over Europe. The North Sea Jazz Festival is world-renowned and features a dazzling array of musical genres ranging from traditional New Orleans jazz to swing, bebop, hardbop, free jazz, fusion, jazz-rock, blues, gospel, funk, soul, hiphop, jazzdance, and drum 'n bass. Consequently, many of the big names in music have performed at the festival, including Ella Fitzgerald, Al Jarreau, Lionel Hampton, B. B. King, and the Art Ensemble of Chicago.

Below: **The first North Sea Festival, held in The Hague, drew performances by legendary jazz artists such as Sarah Vaughan, Count Basie, Dizzy Gillespie, and Stan Getz. Here, Vaughan *(center)* and Gillespie *(right)* strike a comic pose with jazz artist Roy Eldridge *(left)*.**

Famous Dutch-Americans

Three former U.S. presidents — Martin Van Buren (1782–1862), Theodore Roosevelt (1858–1919), and Franklin Delano Roosevelt (1882–1945) — were of Dutch descent. Van Buren is best remembered for his campaign against slavery, while Theodore Roosevelt won the Nobel Peace Prize in 1906 for mediating an end to the Russo-Japanese War (1904–1905). Franklin Roosevelt guided the country through World War II. Admired by the American people, the three men were firm believers in democracy and equality for all.

Today, the Roosevelt Study Center in Middelburg, Netherlands, permanently features an exhibition on the lives and achievements of Theodore, Franklin, and Eleanor Roosevelt, whose ancestors came from Zeeland. The study center also acts as a primary research institute, conference center, and library on twentieth century American history. The study center is partly funded by the province of Zeeland, the Royal Netherlands Academy of Arts and Sciences, and private Dutch corporations. The center works closely with the Theodore Roosevelt Association and the Franklin and Eleanor Roosevelt Institute in New York.

Opposite: **Titled *Woman I*, this painting is a work of Willem de Kooning (1904–1997). In 1926, Kooning moved to the United States, where he worked as a house painter and a commercial painter before becoming famous. In the 1930s, he created murals for the Federal Arts Project. His black-and-white abstract paintings made him one of the leading figures of the New York School of Abstract Expressionism. His two most outstanding works are *Asheville* in the Phillips Collection, Washington, D.C., and *Excavation* at the Art Institute of Chicago.**

Peter Minuit (1580–1638)

Minuit was born a Walloon (a Belgian, French-speaking Protestant) in Germany. Worried that the Spanish authorities were going to persecute them for religious reasons, his family fled to the Netherlands when he was a small boy. Minuit grew up to become an employee of the Dutch West India Company and arrived at the mouth of the Hudson River in 1626 to take up his assignment as the first director of the New Netherland colony.

Shortly after he arrived, war broke out between the Mohawks and Mohicans. Anxious that the Dutch settlers in the more remote parts of the colony were unsafe, he directed them to relocate in what is today Manhattan, an area mostly deserted by the American Indians at that time. To strengthen control over the island, Minuit purchased Manhattan, possibly the most valuable real estate in the world today, from the Lenapes, or Indians of the Delaware region, for 60 guilders (U.S. $25). The newly purchased land was named New Amsterdam. Minuit served as director of the colony until 1633. Today, Minuit's historical purchase is depicted on the granite base of a flagstaff in Battery Park.

Above: **Peter Minuit is also remembered by the Peter Minuit Plaza in New York and the Peter Minuit School, a public school on Madison Avenue in New York City.**

Dutch People in Canada

Relations between the Netherlands and Canada, while friendly, did not flourish until World War II. During the war, Princess Juliana, later queen of the Netherlands, and her family were offered shelter by the Canadian government while their country was occupied by the Nazis. Unlike the United States, Canada did not receive many Dutch immigrants until the years following World War II. A mutually fulfilling arrangement led to more Dutch people moving to Canada. Many Dutch people, devastated by the war, were looking for a better life outside the country, and Canada needed farm workers for the many farms abandoned by their native owners, who had gone to war and died. More than 100,000 Dutch immigrants entered Canada in the period between 1947 and 1960. After 1960, Dutch immigration dropped drastically because the Netherlands itself was experiencing great economic expansion. Most Dutch-Canadians reside in Ontario, British Columbia, and Alberta. A significant number of Dutch-Canadians live in southwestern Ontario. Cities, such as Toronto and Vancouver, also support large populations of Dutch-Canadians. The Dutch form the seventh largest ethnic group in Canada.

Left: **Based in Guelph, Ontario, John Boers, 65, specializes in reuniting Dutch-Canadian World War II veterans with their Dutch families. Large parts of Europe were destroyed by war, many soldiers were unable to locate their families or loved ones in the period of chaos that followed the end of World War II.**

Ottawa — Tulip Capital of North America

Although the Dutch-American and Dutch-Canadian communities organize tulip festivals in different parts of North America during spring, the largest tulip festival in the world is held in Ottawa, Canada. In the fall of 1945, Princess Juliana presented Ottawa with 100,000 tulip bulbs, a gesture of gratitude to the Canadian government for sheltering her family during World War II and to the Canadian troops that fought for the liberation of the Netherlands. The bulbs flourished in Canadian soil and climate, growing so well that the capital region became the "Tulip Capital of North America" in just a few years. The first Canadian Tulip Festival was held in 1953 in Ottawa and has since grown into Canada's most colorful event. Drawing tulip enthusiasts from North America, Europe, and Asia, the festival also includes concerts, parades, and strolls through the tulip gardens.

Dutch Embassy and Consulates in Canada

The Dutch government has numerous Canadian offices. Led by ambassador D. J. van Houten, the Dutch embassy is located in Ottawa, and eleven consulates are located throughout Canada, including one each in Toronto, Montreal, Winnipeg, and Québec.

Above: As part of the Canadian Tulip Festival, yachts that have been decorated with tulips sail through the Rideau Canal in Ottawa each year.

Below: Photographers from all over the world gather at the tulip festival in Ottawa to capture rare scenes of color and beauty.

The Netherlands map with grid columns A, B, C, D and rows 1, 2, 3, 4, 5.

Legend:
- Province Boundary
- ■ Capital
- ● City
- River
- Dam

N

WADDEN ISLANDS

Terschelling *Ameland* *Schiermonnikoog*

Vlieland Wadden Sea

GRONINGEN

Texel ●Groningen

Leeuwarden●

FRIESLAND

DRENTHE

NORTH

SEA

IJsselmeer

NOORD-HOLLAND

●Staphorst

Alkmaar● Rouveen●

●Edam **OVERIJSSEL**

Marken **FLEVOLAND**

Haarlem● *IJssel*

AMSTERDAM■ *Amstel*

Aalsmeer● Apeldoorn●

●Baarn

●Leiden **GELDERLAND**

RANDSTAD **UTRECHT**

The Hague● Utrecht●

Delft● Arnhem●

Europoort Gouda● *Waal*

Haringvliet Dam Rotterdam● Nijmegen●

Kinderdijk●

Maas *Rhine*

Storm Surge Barrier *Philips Dam*

Veere● **East Schelde** **NOORD-BRABANT** **GERMANY**

●Middelburg Tilburg●

ZEELAND

West Schelde Eindhoven●

Schelde **LIMBURG**

BELGIUM

THE
NETHERLANDS

Maastricht●

▲*Vaalserberg*
(1,053 ft / 321 m)

Above: This little girl tries unsuccessfully to walk in a pair of vastly oversized clogs.

THE
NETHERLANDS

How Is Your Geography?

Learning to identify the main geographical areas and points of a country can be challenging. Although it may seem difficult at first to memorize the locations and spellings of major cities or the names of mountain ranges, rivers, deserts, lakes, and other prominent physical features, the end result of this effort can be very rewarding. Places you previously did not know existed will suddenly come to life when referred to in world news, whether in newspapers, television reports, or other books and reference sources. This knowledge will make you feel a bit closer to the rest of the world, with its fascinating variety of cultures and physical geography.

Used in a classroom setting, the instructor can make duplicates of this map using a copy machine. (PLEASE DO NOT WRITE IN THIS BOOK!) Students can then fill in any requested information on their individual map copies. Used one-on-one, the student can also make copies of the map on a copy machine and use them as a study tool. The student can practice identifying place names and geographical features on his or her own.

Below: **The settlement along this harbor on the island of Marken is known as the museum village.**

The Netherlands at a Glance

Official Name	Kingdom of the Netherlands
Capital	Amsterdam
Official Language	Dutch
Population	15.9 million
Land Area	16,031 square miles (41,532 square kilometers)
Coastline	280 miles (451 km)
Provinces	Drenthe, Flevoland, Friesland, Gelderland, Groningen, Limburg, Noord-Brabant, Noord-Holland, Overijssel, Utrecht, Zeeland, Zuid-Holland.
Highest Point	Vaalserberg (1,053 feet/321 meters)
Major Rivers	Maas, IJessel, Rhine, Schelde, Waal
Major Religion	Christianity (Roman Catholic and Protestant)
National Anthem	*Wilhelmus van Nassouwe*
National Flower	Tulip
Holidays	New Year (January 1)
	Carnival (February/March)
	Windmill Day (May)
	Sinterklaas (December 5)
	Queensday (April 30)
Famous Leaders	William I of Orange-Nassau (1533–1584)
	Johan de Wit (1625–1672)
	J. R. Thorbecke (1798–1872)
	Queen Wilhelmina (1880–1962)
Currency	Guilders (U.S. $1 = NLG 2.38)

Opposite: **These two porters in Alkmaar are carrying big disks of Gouda out of the weighing house.**

Glossary

Dutch Vocabulary

boterletter (boh-ter-LET-ter): a puff pastry filled with almond paste.

Elfstedentocht (elf-STAY-den-tokt): "Eleven Towns Race;" a marathon skating race in Friesland covering a distance of 125 miles (200 kilometers) across eleven towns.

fierljeppen (feerl-YEP-pen): pole-vaulting over a canal or ditch; a sport played in Friesland.

rijstaffel (RICE-tah-fel): a meal of rice served with an array of up to thirty dishes and hot sauce on the side.

sate (SAH-tay): grilled skewers of meat accompanied by a spicy peanut sauce.

Sinterklaas (SIN-ter-klahs): the Dutch name for Saint Nicholas, patron saint of sailors and of the city of Amsterdam; the main festival in honor of Sinterklaas is celebrated on December 5.

stadholder (STAD-hoh-der): governor of a province.

surprises (sir-PREEZ-us): gifts for adults during Sinterklaas, usually accompanied with a poem.

wadlopen (vad-LOH-pun): mud flat walking, which is a popular sport on the coasts of Friesland and Groningen.

Zwarte Piet (zwar-tah PEET): "Black Peter;" a helper of Sinterklaas.

English Vocabulary

allotments: small areas of public land rented out for cultivation.

amphibian: animals that can live both on land and in water.

anonymously: with a name that is not known or made public.

appropriate: relevant or suitable.

aristocracy: the nobility or upper classes who usually rule a country.

carillons: musical instruments consisting of sets of stationary bells rung either manually or with a pedal.

coalition: the temporary union of several political parties for political purposes, usually to win the election.

collaborate: to cooperate with an enemy occupying one's country.

compulsory: mandatory; a must.

constitutional monarchy: a type of government in which the power of the king or sovereign ruler is defined by the laws of an established constitution.

councillor pensionary: prime minister of the States-General in the days of the United Provinces of the Netherlands.

debacle: disaster or complete failure.

delta: a triangular patch of land made up of sediment accumulated at the mouth of a river, usually situated between two or more of the river's branches.

diametrically opposed: describing two persons or objects that are opposite extremes or in direct opposition.

egalitarian: subscribing to the principle that all people are equal, especially in society, politics, and economics.

encroaching: intruding or advancing beyond the original limits.

enshrined: greatly valued or cherished as sacred.

estuaries: the tidal mouths of large rivers.

favoritism: the unfair preference for one person or group at the expense of another.

femme fatale: a beautiful or charming woman who often leads men into danger or disaster.

flamboyant: excessively ornate or elaborately styled.

formalism: the strict observance of traditions, customs, or rituals.

gable: the front part of a house that is just under the roof and is usually triangular in shape.

glimpse: a brief view.

Gothic: a style of architecture that was popular between the twelfth and sixteenth centuries and characterized by pointed or ribbed arches as well as rich ornamentation.

grotesque: odd or unnatural in shape and usually ugly.

guttural: describing throaty or harsh sounds, often made from the back of the mouth or throat.

heretical: relating to religious beliefs that differ from a church's doctrine.

inhabitable: describing a place or building suitable for people to reside in or occupy.

integrity: a sense of honesty and incorruptibility.

land reclamation: the act or process of converting wetlands, wastelands, or otherwise unusable areas into dry, usable, and productive land.

medieval: describing or belonging to the Middle Ages, a historical period extending from about A.D. 500 to about 1500.

modernist: (adj.) using modern ideas or methods; reflecting a conscious break with the past and a search for new forms of expression.

notorious: widely and unfavorably known.

ostentatious: conspicuous or pretentious; marked by a desire to attract attention or impress others.

outskirts: the outer districts or outlying parts of a town.

phenomenon: a rare or significant fact or occurrence as perceived by the senses or by the mind.

polders: areas of reclaimed land protected by dikes.

reviving: bringing back to life or consciousness.

sedentary: requiring little or no activity or exercise.

States-General: the Dutch Parliament, which consists of an upper and a lower house

synonymous: sharing the same or almost the same meaning.

tableau: a striking or artistic grouping of people, objects, etc., arranged to represent a scene.

tint: a slight trace of a different color.

unaffiliated: not associated, connected, or related to any organization or person.

utilitarian: guided or abiding by the fundamental principle of utilitarianism. Utilitarianism consists of the pursuit of the greatest happiness for the greatest number of people.

zest: hearty enjoyment or relish.

More Books to Read

Amsterdam. Cities of the World series. Deborah Kent (Children's Press)

Anne Frank. First Book series. Rachel Epstein (Franklin Watts)

Netherlands. Cultures of the World series. Pat Seward (Benchmark Books)

The Netherlands. Enchantment of the World second series. Martin Hintz (Children's Press)

Netherlands. Festivals of the World series. Joyce Van Fenema (Gareth Stevens)

The Netherlands. Major World Nations series. Ronald Seth (Chelsea House)

Rembrandt: Life of a Portrait Painter. Great Artists series. David Spence (Barrons Educational Series)

Van Gogh. Eyewitness series. Bruce Bernard (DK Publishing)

Videos

The Back Roads of Europe — Italy, France, Spain, Germany, Austria, England, and the Netherlands. (BFS Entertainment & Multimedia)

Biography — Vincent Van Gogh: A Stroke of Genius. (A & E Entertainment)

Low Countries: Holland, Belgium, and Luxembourg. (Questar)

Royal Families of the World: Great Britain, Sweden, Netherlands, Belgium. (Goldhil Home Media)

Web Sites

www.the-netherlands.com

www.netherlands-embassy.org/fie_country.html

www.annefrank.nl/eng/afh/afh.html

www.visitholland.com/

www.ibiblio.org/wm/paint/auth/rembrandt/

Due to the dynamic nature of the Internet, some web sites stay current longer than others. To find additional web sites, use a reliable search engine with one or more of the following keywords to help you locate information about the Netherlands. Keywords: *Amsterdam, Dutch history, van Gogh, Holland, polders, Rembrandt, tulips, windmills.*

Index